The Solution
Selling
Fieldbook

**Keith M. Eades
James N. Touchstone
Timothy T. Sullivan**

McGraw-Hill

New York   Chicago   San Francisco
Lisbon   London   Madrid   Mexico City   Milan
New Delhi   San Juan   Seoul   Singapore
Sydney   Toronto

Copyright © 2005 by Solution Selling Inc. All rights reserved. Printed in the United States of America. Except as permitted under the United States Copyright Act of 1976, no part of this publication may be reproduced or distributed in any form or by any means, or stored in a data base or retrieval system, without the prior written permission of the publisher.

6 7 8 9 0 DOC/DOC 0 9

ISBN 0-07-145608-2
part of ISBN 0-07-145607-4

This publication is designed to provide accurate and authoritative information in regard to the subject matter covered. It is sold with the understanding that neither the author nor the publisher is engaged in rendering legal, accounting, or other professional service. If legal advice or other expert assistance is required, the services of a competent professional person should be sought.

> —*From a declaration of principles jointly adopted by a committee of the American Bar Association and a committee of publishers.*

McGraw-Hill books are available at special quantity discounts to use as premiums and sales promotions, or for use in corporate training programs. For more information, please write to the Director of Special Sales, Professional Publishing, McGraw-Hill, Two Penn Plaza, New York, NY 10121-2298. Or contact your local bookstore.

Library of Congress Cataloging-in-Publication Data

Eades, Keith M.
  The solution selling fieldbook : practical tools, application exercises, templates, and scripts for effective sales execution / by Keith Eades and James N. Touchstone.
    p. cm.
  ISBN 0-07-145607-4 (hardcover : alk. paper)
  1. Selling—Handbooks, manuals, etc. 2. Sales management—Handbooks, manuals, etc. 3. Six sigma (Quality control standard)—Handbooks, manuals, etc. I. Touchstone, James N. II. Title.

  HF5438.25.E19 2005
  658.8′101—dc22
  3990   200500

CONTENTS

NOTE: The Solution Selling Job Aid Icons Flow Model can be found between pages 182 and 183.

PART THREE
Engaging in Active Opportunities

PART FOUR
Qualifying, Controlling, and Closing Opportunities

PART FIVE
Managing Your Opportunities

PART SIX
Solution Selling Reference Section

INTRODUCTION

According to the U.S. Census and Department of Labor statistics, almost one-fifth of the American workforce, more than 25 million people, is formally employed as salespeople. The number of professional salespeople all over the world is not precisely known, but it's a sure bet that it exceeds hundreds of millions.

Despite the huge numbers of people who make a living by selling goods and services to other people, sales techniques have typically been learned "on the job." Selling has always been regarded as more of an art than a science. There have been very limited resources for helping sales professionals to master their craft.

The old cliché of salespeople as "silver-tongued devils" is rapidly fading away. Thank goodness—that outdated Hollywood stereotype of salespeople as generally devious and untrustworthy hucksters is an utterly inaccurate picture of the millions of sales professionals all over the world.

To succeed in today's highly competitive global market, sales professionals can't get away with manipulative tricks or high-pressure tactics, nor can they rely solely upon their good looks and charm to woo buyers. Instead, sales professionals must provide real service to their customers—they have to understand buyers' needs, diagnose their problems, and prescribe authentic solutions that deliver substantial value.

Customers now demand an ever-rising standard of performance from the people from whom they buy. Today, if a buyer interacts with you, that buyer expects you to give him or her value starting with the very first call. Buyers have more information available to them than ever before, and they are able to communicate faster and more effectively. They can evaluate options rapidly and get accurate prices and specifications from multiple sources quickly. In fact, for many commodity purchases, buyers have found ways to dispense with salespeople altogether by buying what they need electronically. This purchasing approach is a growing trend faced by many sales organizations.

To succeed in today's demanding marketplace, not only must you have exceptional interpersonal relationship and communications skills, but you must also provide valuable knowledge, experience, and expertise to buyers. Selling as a pure art form is giving way to selling as a science—while still leaving some room for creativity.

For this reason, the Solution Selling methodology was created. Based upon how buyers buy and effective practices of the world's most successful sales professionals, Solution Selling provides a way to meet buyers' demanding requirements, not only with *what* you sell, but, more importantly, by the *way* that you sell, too. *The Solution Selling Fieldbook* will show you how.

About This Book

Welcome to *The Solution Selling Fieldbook*. This book is a "how to" guide that complements my previous book, *The New Solution Selling: The Revolutionary Sales Process That Is Changing the Way People Sell* (ISBN: 0-07-143539-5, published by McGraw-Hill, 2004), which describes the world's most widely used sales execution methodology. In this book, I explain all the practical aspects of putting the Solution Selling methodology into practice.

This book is called a "fieldbook" because I want you to use it in the field, applying its contents to real opportunities to help your buyers get the solutions they need, and to help you live a more productive and personally rewarding life. The methods, processes, tools, job aids, and techniques contained in this book have been tested and proven by more than 500,000 sales professionals all over the world competing in virtually every industry. It contains all you need to know to win more business for yourself and your organization.

While my previous book described the philosophy, theory, and doctrine of the Solution Selling methodology, this book focuses instead on practical application of the methodology's principles to your sales situations. This fieldbook will not dwell on *why* Solution Selling works—for those reasons, see the earlier book. Instead, it will focus on *how* you can apply Solution Selling to produce more sales, and at the same time create happier and more satisfied customers.

Who Needs to Read This Book?

As you might expect, sales professionals will find the contents of this book invaluable. However, selling is becoming more of a team sport every day. I wrote *The Solution Selling Fieldbook* not only for salespeople who want to learn more effective ways to succeed in their job, but also for people who can benefit from understanding what it takes to succeed in sales, including

- *Marketing professionals* The Solution Selling methodology includes job aids and tools that provide marketers with a unique opportunity to align with their sales team. By understanding Solution Selling, they can equip their organization's salespeople with the right messages for the right buyers at the right time and, in turn, achieve their own marketing objectives more easily.

- *Sales support specialists* Many companies hire subject matter experts who understand the details of a particular product or service, or who have expertise in a specific industry, to support salespeople in diagnosing buyer needs, demonstrating the value of your offerings, or other sales-related activities. Although they may not be responsible for closing sales opportunities, sales support specialists play a key role in winning many complex sales campaigns. These professionals can benefit from understanding how they can apply the Solution Selling methodology, which will improve their performance.

- *Management and executives* If you are a manager in your organization, even if your department isn't sales, you can benefit from knowing how to support your organization's sales efforts. Almost anyone in any organization can either impede or assist the organization's sales team. If you are in finance or administration, for example, knowing how your department's policies align with an effective sales process can make a huge difference in your sales team's success—and as a result, in your organization's collective success as well.

- *Partners and alliances* Many companies form partnerships or alliances with third-party organizations so that they can provide better solutions to joint customers. An understanding of the Solution Selling methodology will help you to sell those partnered offerings more effectively, which in turn makes you a more valuable partner or ally, resulting in increased business for you and your organization.

If your personal success is dependent upon either your ability or your organization's ability to sell, then this book is for you. In other words, just about anyone will find benefit from reading *The Solution Selling Fieldbook* and deploying its elements.

In fact, many people have applied Solution Selling principles to improve their personal as well as their professional lives. The next time you have a disagreement with a family member or friend, try using some aspects of Solution Selling to diagnose the situation and resolve the matter. Many times, succeeding in life is really about helping someone to buy into solutions that benefit both of you, after all.

ACKNOWLEDGMENTS

This fieldbook is a result of the creativity, experience, and efforts of many people. I want to specifically thank Jim Touchstone and Tim Sullivan for assisting me in the authorship and direction of this fieldbook. I appreciate their time and effort, but even more their passion and attention in creating a fieldbook that will truly benefit our clients.

For the last 10 years, Jim Touchstone has traveled the world, working with a variety of clients to customize, teach, implement, and reinforce the elements of Solution Selling. Jim is currently responsible for making sure that the Solution Selling methodology is both current and relevant across multiple industry sectors. Not only is he is intimately familiar with the methodology, he understands how to apply it in everyday life.

I've known and worked with Tim Sullivan for more than 25 years. He impresses me daily with his deep understanding and working knowledge of sales methodologies. In my estimation, Tim is one of the world's foremost experts in the field. Prior to joining me at SPI, Tim played an instrumental role at Siebel/

OnTarget, where he helped develop and implement Target Account Selling (TAS) with multiple clients throughout the world.

Special thanks to Jeffrey Krames, our publisher at McGraw-Hill, to the talented and dedicated staff at Sales Performance International, our Solution Selling Business Partners, and certainly to our clients. Their spirit and contributions over the years have helped shape much of the content of this fieldbook.

And finally, I know I speak for all three of us when I say thank you for the support we have received from our families. I thank my wife, Margie, and my sons, Michael, John, and David; Jim thanks his wife, Kelley; Tim thanks his wife, Jane, and his daughters, Erin and Shannon.

GETTING STARTED

CHAPTER 1

HOW TO USE THIS FIELDBOOK

Sharpen your pencils. The *Solution Selling Fieldbook* was designed to be written in, marked up, noted upon, and used. Use a pen or highlighter to mark phrases or sections that you find especially useful for your situations. I've left margins wide enough for you to make your own personal notes, too. Fold down the corners of the pages that you want to refer to, or stick reminder notes on parts that you find most useful.

This fieldbook includes numerous practical exercises to help you understand key concepts and apply them to your sales situations. I urge you to complete the exercises. This will enable you to put Solution Selling into practice. Practice makes perfect—if you just read the chapters and don't do the exercises, you won't get a complete understanding of how to use Solution Selling in the real world.

At the back of the book, you'll find a CD-ROM that includes the Solution Selling job aids in the Microsoft Word format. This will allow you to start using these templates very quickly on your own computer. The CD-ROM also contains a free trial version of Solution Selling Software, an application that supports use of the methodology. If you prefer to use good old-fashioned pen and paper, see Appendix B, "Solution Selling Job Aid Templates." This section contains a complete set of job aid templates for your own personal use.

A Note about Copyright

I encourage you to use all of the materials contained in this fieldbook to help you with your personal sales efforts. However, please do not copy any portion of this book for use by others, for resale, or for other commercial purposes without the express written consent of Sales Performance International. The content of this book is protected by copyright laws and is not released for free use in the public domain.

In other words, if you have a friend or coworker who wants to use the materials in your copy of *The Solution Selling Fieldbook*, tell that person to buy his or her own copy, or, better yet, buy a copy and present it to that person as a gift.

Navigating the Fieldbook

This fieldbook is organized into six parts, and each part is divided into several chapters. Here is a quick overview of each part, so that you can turn to the chapters that interest you most.

Part One: Getting Started

You're reading the first chapter of this part right now. In this part, I describe how best to use this book so that you can get the best results. For those who have not yet read *The New Solution Selling* or haven't attended a Solution Selling workshop, let me encourage you to do so. If this fieldbook is your first exposure to Solution Selling, then be sure to read Chapter 2, "Solution Selling Overview," which summarizes important aspects of the methodology.

Part Two: Creating New Opportunities

This part describes how to pursue new sales opportunities with prospective buyers who are not yet aware that they need the capabilities that you or your organization provides. Uncovering these *latent opportunities* is an extremely powerful component of the Solution Selling methodology. Once these opportunities are initiated, they provide you with the highest probability of winning.

Part Three: Engaging in Active Opportunities

This part describes how to qualify and pursue competitive sales opportunities when you are not first. Winning these *active opportunities* requires actions that are quite different from those used to win latent opportunities. Reengineering the buyer's vision of a potential solution to one that favors you is required.

Part Four: Qualifying, Controlling, and Closing Opportunities

This part describes important methods for gaining access to powerful people in the buying organization, controlling the buying process, selling value, and reaching final agreement with the buyer. It also covers often overlooked ways to measure the value delivered to customers, and how to leverage that success into repeat sales.

Part Five: Managing Your Opportunities

This part describes ways in which you can manage your sales pipeline, so that you can maintain a consistent revenue stream and predict future sales accurately.

Part Six: Solution Selling Reference Section

At the end of the book, you'll find appendices containing information that describes what is on the accompanying CD-ROM and how to use it, as well as a section that provides descriptions and templates for all the Solution Selling job aids.

Icons Used in This Book

Some of the information in the fieldbook is accompanied by special icons to call your attention to important points and to make them easier for you to find later. Here is a description of what each icon means:

 Every time you see this icon, it represents a *Solution Selling basic principle*.

 When you see this icon, it refers to a *Solution Selling job aid*—a template or tool that can assist you in completing a sales activity.

 This icon highlights information about the *scalability of Solution Selling* to different types of sales situations, from complex to simple transactions.

Additionally, you'll find a map indicating how to use the job aids introduced in each chapter within the context of the sales process. See the Solution Selling Job Aid Icons Flow Model located in the middle of this book.

Where to Go from Here

If you're not familiar with the Solution Selling methodology and sales process, then I recommend that you read the book sequentially from front to back. The methodology and sales process builds upon itself, one step at a time. You need to understand the initial concepts to know how to use some of the later ones.

If you've already read *The New Solution Selling*, or if you've attended a Solution Selling workshop, then much of this book will read like a review with a strong emphasis on application. In this case, I encourage you to review the section of this chapter "Navigating the Fieldbook," browse the table of contents, and then go straight to the application exercises within each chapter.

Good luck and good selling!

CHAPTER 2

SOLUTION SELLING OVERVIEW

What is solution selling?

Solution Selling is a sales process. It's the most widely used sales process focused on executable selling in the world today. More than 500,000 individuals have been trained in Solution Selling and use components of it every day to assist them in their selling activities.

Executable selling activities involve direct contact with prospective buyers. For many individuals and companies, Solution Selling is the total end-to-end sales process. For others with more complex sales situations, it's the executable portion of the selling process. Solution Selling not only helps with what to do, but specifically focuses on how to do it.

The Solution Selling sales process consists of the following components: a philosophy, a map, a methodology, and a sales management system.

It's a Philosophy

The customer is the focal point. Helping customers solve their business problems and achieve positive, measurable results is the basis of all actions. The steps in the Solution Selling sales process are aligned with how buyers buy.

It's a Map

Solution Selling provides a map of how to get from where you are to where you want to be. Solution Selling provides an end-to-end series of next steps to follow. *End-to-end* means from the beginning of a sale right through to winning it. This includes pre-call planning and research, stimulating interest, diagnosing problems, vision processing, controlling the sale, closing, and measuring success. It includes the ability to identify, analyze, report on, and self-manage individual opportunities using the process. It also provides the ability to predict sales performance success or failure.

It's a Methodology

Solution Selling is a collection of methods that includes tools, job aids, techniques, and procedures that help you or members of your team navigate the selling steps that close more sales faster. It results in higher levels of customer satisfaction and increased sales productivity.

It's a Sales Management System

Solution Selling provides the individual salesperson, as well as sales and executive management, with a process for analyzing pipelines, qualifying opportunities, and coaching skills, thus increasing productivity and predictability. It results in a high-performance sales culture.

The Solution Selling Process Flow Model

The process flow model was developed to help individuals learn the Solution Selling process. The Solution Selling process flow model results from identifying the steps that align with how buyers buy. It helps anyone involved in the sale to visualize where he or she is and what he or she needs to do next with an opportunity. The steps also provide a reasonable definition of each person's responsibility.

In this era of selling, a sale is often a team sale. For example, a telemarketer, marketing professional, or "inside" rep may conduct pre-call planning and research, stimulate interest, and discover pain, as well as field inbound calls from prospective buyers. Once opportunities have been <u>qualified</u>, they may be handed over to someone in a traditional sales role, such as a salesperson, account manager, or "outside" rep, for vision processing and gaining access to power. This person may carry the opportunity to closure or bring in a business partner or project team to help manage an evaluation plan through to closure.

If necessary, organizations and individuals will have to decide the roles and handoffs required of each sales professional. Regardless of one's role, the chapters of this fieldbook are designed to help the reader hone and execute the skills needed within each step. Often I will use the term *salesperson* generically to refer to any of the sales-related professionals just mentioned.

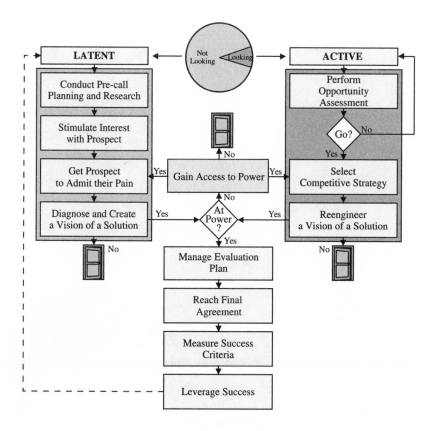

The Solution Selling Sales Process

As indicated in the Solution Selling process flow model, a clear line of distinction is made between opportunities that you initiate and opportunities that are already active that find you. These are two very different starting points for sales opportunities. In this fieldbook, we'll conduct exercises for both latent and active situations.

Starting from the top, the process flow model is divided into two parts: to the left are latent pain opportunities (people who are not looking to buy anything from you or anyone else), and to the right are active opportunities (people who are already looking to buy and most likely have a vision of what they need—and that vision probably doesn't include you).

Latent Opportunities

These opportunities arise from helping prospective buyers recognize a pain that they have not been dealing with. Through either ignorance or rationalization, they have decided to live with the problem. Salespeople often avoid developing latent opportunities because they think it takes too long—or because they simply don't know how.

In Part Two, "Creating New Opportunities," you will apply concepts and exercises to a potential opportunity of yours around the topics:

- *How to conduct effective pre-call planning and research* Access pertinent information about prospect organizations in order to uncover likely pains that will be of high priority to resolve. Identify the person within the prospect organization who might serve as the optimal entry point.

- *How to stimulate interest with prospects* Incorporate messages into your approach for stimulating interest that center around pain and describe how peers of the prospect have already solved similar business issues with your help.

- *How to help prospects admit pain* Position and align your selling activities in a manner that will allow the prospect to conclude that you are sincere and competent. Once you are viewed as trustworthy, sharing results-oriented success stories of your clients with the prospect can help lead to the prospect's admission of pain. Give pain to get pain.

- *How to diagnose and create a vision of solution* Upon the admission of pain, ask diagnostic questions that will help lead the prospect to a self-conclusion of how to solve the pain. This diagnosis should occur before you introduce your products or services.

Active Opportunities

Look at the right-hand side of the model, or active opportunities. These are opportunities that you didn't create. They might have come from an incoming phone call, a formal RFP (request for proposal), or an RFI (request for information). The critical point is that the buyer has found you.

In Part Three, "Engaging in Active Opportunities," you will apply concepts and exercises to a potential opportunity of yours around the topics:

- *How to conduct an opportunity assessment* Determine whether or not you should engage in the opportunity based on an objective, standard set of qualification criteria that gauges the actions of a buyer, not just their words.

- *How to determine which strategy to compete with* Answer key questions to determine which of five primary competitive strategies and supporting tactics to utilize for a given opportunity.

- *How to reengineer a vision of a solution* Lead the prospect to a self-conclusion that it is necessary to change or expand the existing vision of a solution to one favorable to your products or services. You should attempt to introduce differentiating capabilities in order to reengineer an existing vision.

Qualify, Control, and Close

Regardless of whether you have created a new opportunity or engaged in an active one, once the prospect has a buying vision that is biased toward your offerings, you should begin to qualify, control, and close the opportunity.

In Part Four, "Qualifying, Controlling, and Closing Opportunities," you will apply concepts and exercises to a potential opportunity around these topics:

- *How to gain access to power* If you are unable to call directly on a prospective buyer who has the influence or authority to make a purchasing decision, you should work with a sponsor to get to the person who does. If necessary, negotiate proof of capabilities with your sponsor in exchange for access to power.

- *How to control the buying process* Uncover, influence, and lead the steps of the power sponsor's buying and evaluation process. Develop a mutual plan that leads to a buying decision.

- *How to sell with value* Demonstrate and deliver value throughout the life cycle of your opportunity. Lead with value to start a sell cycle, verify the value during the sell cycle, close with value at the end of the sell cycle, and measure the value on an ongoing basis.

- *How to reach final agreement* Anticipate the concessions your buyer will ask for in advance and prepare a list of items that you may be willing to concede. Prepare negotiation stands that are based upon your working knowledge of the buyer's situation and the value you bring to the table.

- *How to measure and leverage success* Establish success criteria with the customer. Periodically measure the results in order to ensure the desired outcomes and leverage positive results to stimulate interest in future opportunities.

Applying the Fieldbook Exercises— Something for Everyone

The exercises in the fieldbook are designed to help you plan for and execute the steps of the sales process. If you are a salesperson, you may find it useful to apply the exercises and job aids to an important opportunity that you are trying to win. If you are not in a direct sales position or don't have an opportunity to work through the model, you may want to approach the exercises with a general sales scenario in mind. This general sales scenario approach will allow you to navigate the entire sales process.

Regardless of your approach, let's get started.

CREATING NEW OPPORTUNITIES

CHAPTER 3

HOW TO CONDUCT EFFECTIVE PRE-CALL PLANNING AND RESEARCH

Why is pre-call planning and research important?

Often, after losing a game, you'll hear professional athletes utter this cliché: "It was a perfect game plan, just poorly executed." After losing a sale, you may hear salespeople use a variant of the old sports adage: "It was a good plan, just poorly executed."

To win in sales, sports, or any endeavor, proper preparation is the key. Think about your favorite professional athlete or stage performer. How many hours a week does that person prepare before a big game or major performance? The ratio of practice time to game time is probably something in excess of 10:1— often much more.

But how much do sales, marketing, or other business professionals prepare prior to interacting with prospective buyers? Many admit that their ratio of preparation time to actual meeting time is frequently much less than 1:1. The result of this poor preparation is virtually always poor performance.

Executing winning sales depends on the effectiveness of the planning and research that takes place prior to talking with prospective buyers. As described in *The New Solution Selling*, the common denominator of effective pre-call planning and research is "a focus on identifying potential pains."

What is "pain"? In Solution Selling, pain refers to a critical business issue or potential missed opportunity—something that motivates a buyer to act.

In this chapter, you'll find useful principles, exercises, and job aids that help to identify potential pains. Those Solution Selling job aids are the

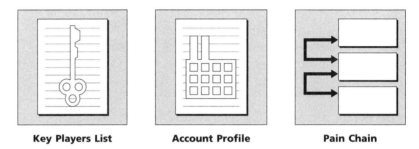

Key Players List   **Account Profile**   **Pain Chain**

Why is the identification of pain so important? Without pain, buyers have no reason to change. This takes us to the first basic principle of Solution Selling.

BASIC PRINCIPLE

NO PAIN, NO CHANGE

In Solution Selling, "no pain, no change" is the foundational principle upon which all the other principles of an effective sales process are built. The word *pain* serves to emphasize this point: Buyers are most motivated to act when their problems are both painful and very personal.

Those sales professionals who claim that they focus on "needs selling" are on the right track. They focus on the needs of buyers instead of solely on what they have to sell. But there is something that precedes buyer need: the critical business issue that caused the buyer to analyze just what is needed in the first place.

Whatever you call it—a business driver, a compelling reason to act, a problem, a potential missed opportunity, a critical business issue, or quite simply a pain—buyers will not take action without one. In other words, no pain, no change.

Although the concept that people buy things in order to solve problems seems straightforward, many salespeople never uncover the underlying problems or pains that drive prospective buyers' actions. Often salespeople assume that buyers can make the connection for themselves on how the offerings solve the pain.

If identifying potential pain is the critical element of effective pre-call planning, then how do you begin? The first step is to identify the key players that you commonly encounter in sales opportunities and record each of their most common pains.

EXERCISE: IDENTIFY POTENTIAL PAINS, PART I

Activities

- List three customer job titles that you commonly encounter in sales opportunities.

- Record three potential pains that each job title is most likely to face.

- Use the worksheet that follows to record your answers.

Identify Potential Pains—Worksheet

Job Title	Potential Pains
	●
	●
	●
	●
	●
	●
	●
	●
	●

To ensure that you have accurately articulated an individual's pain, use the following checklist. At least one of these questions, if not most of them, should be answered yes.

Pain Checklist

Is the pain

❏ Relevant to the role of the individual it corresponds to?

❏ Personal to the individual who owns it?

❏ Something that the individual is measured on?

❏ Something that the individual is motivated to solve?

❏ Something that the individual is rewarded for addressing?

❏ Something the individual is looked to by his or her peers to resolve?

❏ Something that provides the individual a compelling reason to take action?

❐ Articulated in a manner that describes
  ○ Something increasing?
  ○ Something decreasing?
  ○ A compliance that has been mandated?
  ○ A potential missed opportunity?

Pain Examples

- *Increasing* Costs, competitive loses, errors, customer complaints, returns, employee turnover

- *Decreasing* Profits, market share, service, quality, growth rate, customer care

- *Compliance* Government regulation, industry standard

- *Potential missed opportunity* Failed market introduction, wrong market timing

EXERCISE: IDENTIFY POTENTIAL PAINS, PART II

Activities

- Refer to your completed worksheet of potential pains from "Exercise: Identify Potential Pains, Part I."

- Use the pain checklist to ensure that the potential pains you have recorded are accurately articulated.

- Rephrase or delete the recorded potential pains that do not meet any of the pain checklist criteria.

Note: It is important that you complete this exercise, as you will use some of your work in other exercises.

Marketing organizations can help their salespeople's pre-call planning by identifying their target markets, the prospective buyers by job title within those markets, and the high-priority pains that people with those job titles potentially face. The pre-call planning and research job aid used with this activity is called a Key Players List.

Key Players List

Overview

The Key Players List is a listing by industry of important job titles along with the critical business issues (pains) that people with that job title (key players) are likely to face.

Where/How Used

The Key Players List helps you identify pains to probe for when marketing to, calling on, or meeting with a particular buyer based on that buyer's job title and role. This is especially helpful when calling on a buyer or within an industry where you have less experience or that you are unfamiliar with.

The Key Players List can be used to initiate sales opportunities by identifying latent pains that buyers have not yet recognized. It also can be used to identify the underlying pain that has driven a buyer to commit to action in an active sell cycle.

What You Should Achieve

By using the Key Players List, you should be able to identify key players and their potential pains more quickly. This list can also help you develop your situational knowledge and experience in a given industry.

Input Required

To create a Key Players List, you must research the key players, their pains, and their job titles within your target industries.

Note: The ideal situation is to have a database of Key Players Lists for the industries and job titles you typically encounter. These lists should be updated periodically to reflect new information resulting from industry trends and customer interactions.

Before looking at an example of a Key Players List, try the following exercise to see how well you can identify typical pains of different job titles.

EXERCISE: CONNECT THE JOB TITLE TO THE PAIN

Activity

- Using the worksheet that follows, connect each of the job titles to the pain that is most likely to be associated with it.

Notes:

- For this exercise, regard the job titles and pains as pertaining to a general industry.

- As an example, a link has already been made between the Director of Customer Service and her pain of *increasing number of consumer complaints*.

Job Title		**Pain**
A.	Vice President of Application Development	Increasing number of consumer complaints
B.	Chief Executive Officer	Increasing cost of research and design
C.	Vice President of Manufacturing	Increasing equipment maintenance downtime
D.	Chief Operating Officer	Declining value of earnings per share
E.	Vice President of Engineering	Difficulty attracting and hiring new employees
F.	Chief Financial Officer	Missing revenue targets
G.	Vice President of Marketing	New applications are late to market
H.	Director of Customer Service	Increasing cost of staff and operations
I.	Vice President of Human Resources	Declining return on campaigns and promotions
J.	Vice President of Sales	Inability of disparate systems to work together
K.	Information Technology Director	Poor cash flow

Answers: A, new applications are late to market; B, declining value of earnings per share; C, increasing equipment maintenance downtime; D, increasing cost of staff and operations; E, increasing cost of research and design; F, poor cash flow; G, declining return on campaigns and promotions; H, increasing number of consumer complaints; I, difficulty attracting and hiring new employees; J, missing revenue targets; K, inability of disparate systems to work together.

As promised, here is an example of a Key Players List. This one was developed specifically for the manufacturing industry. You can find Key Players Lists for additional industries on the accompanying CD-ROM.

Key Players List—Example

Industry: Manufacturing	
Job Title	**Pains**
Chief Executive Officer	▪ Eroding market share ▪ Not meeting investors' expectations ▪ Declining profitability ▪ Declining shareholder value/earnings per share (EPS)
Chief Operating Officer	▪ Inconsistent quality ▪ Increasing cost of staff ▪ Rising cost of goods sold ▪ Can't meet current customer demands ▪ Falling operating profits ▪ Inability to consistently reach productivity goals
Chief Financial Officer	▪ Lack of timely and accurate reporting ▪ Cash flow problems ▪ Declining return on investment ▪ Declining return on assets
Director of IT/ Vice President of IT	▪ Inability to meet users' demands ▪ Inability to provide long-term strategy ▪ Trouble keeping up with overwhelming technology change ▪ Inability to link disparate systems
Vice President of Manufacturing	▪ Not meeting manufacturing and shipment schedules ▪ Excessive inventory levels ▪ Trouble meeting government regulations ▪ Lack of capital for equipment ▪ Inability to meet cost targets ▪ Increasing equipment maintenance downtime
Vice President of Sales and Marketing	▪ Eroding market share ▪ Poor sales results ▪ Increasing expenses/cost of sales ▪ Inability to forecast revenue accurately ▪ Missed revenue targets ▪ Poor return on marketing campaigns

The Key Players List focuses on the pains of individuals, whereas an Account Profile provides a holistic view of an organization. Analysis of Account Profiles can help uncover potential pains that an organization faces.

Account Profile

Overview
A brief overview of a target company that describes particular elements of the organization. The profile highlights the challenges the organization is facing.

Where/How Used
The Account Profile serves as an ideal "quick information" resource for you to gain insight about an account with which you are about to make contact. The profile should include

- Overview of the company
- Description of its offerings
- Analysis of its markets
- Summary of its financial status
- Description of its competition
- Executive biographies
- Descriptions of potential pains
- Potential capabilities needed

What You Should Achieve
The Account Profile should help you or your team to strategize how to move forward with a potential opportunity by identifying specific pains that the organization is likely to be facing. Additionally, identification of key players within the organization

and their pains will start to formulate a picture of how the individuals' pains are connected in a cause-and-effect relationship.

Input Required

Knowledge of the prospect's organization, the key players, and the pains they are likely to be facing—a Key Players List for the industry will be useful.

Note: Account Profiles can be supplemented by corporate information such as account plans or customer relationship management data. There are also many third-party organizations that can serve as a resource for researching and providing the latest information on accounts. A complete Account Profile represents the minimum amount of information that should be known before engaging with an opportunity.

Account Profiles can be as concise or as lengthy as needed. Six key areas of content and exploration should be the basis for your Account Profiles.

Account Profile Checklist

- ❐ *Overview of the company* Include the company name and a brief description of its primary business. You may want to include the company's mission statement and key facts from its most recent annual report.

- ❐ *Description of its offerings* Describe each significant offering and highlight the key differentiators that provide unique value in the marketplace.

- ❐ *Analysis of its markets* Provide relevant data for the company's position in the marketplace. Include elements such as the company's share of the market, annual revenues, locations, reputation for trends in the market, and maturity of the organization.

- ❐ *Summary of its financial status* Record key information from balance sheets and income statements to see if any trends or track records provide insight into how this company acquires offerings.

❑ *Description of its competition* List the company's primary competitors, how the company compares against the competition from an unbiased market perspective, and common strategies used by the competition.

❑ *Executive biographies, including descriptions of potential pains* Provide information concerning executives' education, work history, track record, intercompany alliances, and relationships as well as recording potential pains they face that may serve as a catalyst for starting a new opportunity.

❑ *Potential capabilities needed* List any of your offerings that may help address the potential pains if they are confirmed to exist.

Today, information is more available to sales organizations than ever before. There are multiple information sources to research to begin to compile Account Profiles. I've listed only a few of those sources here. Some require subscriptions to access certain online sections.

Information Sources for Account Profiles

- *Annual reports* Often annual reports can be obtained online through a company's home page. Both the chairman's letter and the financial highlights/overviews found within the annual reports contain descriptions and expectations for the coming year(s) that can hint at numerous potential initiatives and resulting pains.

- Barron's *or Barron's Online (www.barrons.com)* This source is a weekly business and financial magazine owned by Dow Jones & Company. It too contains useful research capabilities.

- *Hoover's Online (www.hoovers.com)* This online source provides company overviews and information such as financials, key people in the organization, industry-related news, competitor profiles, business and financial rankings, and company subsidiaries. This is a great source for completing most of the minimal requirements of an Account Profile.

- *MSN Business Online (www.msnbc.com)* This online source provides a robust amount of company information and news articles that are searchable at the world, national, and local levels.

- *OneSource (www.onesource.com)* This online resource is literally a single source for detailed company information for both public and private companies. This is also a very good resource for finding accurate information for an Account Profile.

- *Standard & Poor's (www.standardandpoors.com)* This online source provides financial information about organizations around the world in multiple languages. Some of the financial information includes credit ratings, equity research, global indices, and articles pertaining to the financial impact of world events.

- *U.S. Securities & Exchange Commission (www.sec.gov)* This source provides information on public filings from 1993 to the present.

- *Industry periodicals and industry associations.*

- *The company's shareholder department.*

Review the Account Profile example before compiling one yourself.

Account Profile Example

Overview of the company

Titan Games Incorporated (TGI) is a 20-year-old organization that manufactures educational and recreational games and toys and distributes them throughout the world.

Description of its offerings

TGI manufactures a line of educational and recreational games and toys that are endorsed and approved by leading experts in the field. A key differentiator is that TGI's toys are ergonomically designed.

Analysis of its markets

Loss of shelf space has created market erosion and hence a loss of sales, while weakening the company's competitive position.

Summary of its financial status

Sales have declined in direct proportion to market and shelf space loss. Earnings per share have had a disproportionately high decline, as margins are squeezed and costs cannot be reduced quickly enough to protect profits.

Description of its competition

There are five primary competitors, three of which are technologically in a position to take advantage of TGI's inefficiencies.

Executive biographies, including descriptions of potential pains

The CEO, Susan Brown, was hired in the past year to turn the company around because earnings per share have declined. The Vice President of Finance, Jim Smith, has been with TGI for the past five years. He is currently unable to positively affect profits due to missed revenue targets and the increasing cost of credit write-offs. The Vice President of Sales and Marketing, Steve Jones, is charged with increasing TGI's revenues. He has been hampered by technology limitations that cause his salespeople to spend too much time servicing existing accounts instead of developing new ones. The CIO, John Watkins, has been charged with finding a solution to the technology deficiencies.

Potential capabilities needed

TGI appears to need a way for existing customers to place orders directly over the Internet so that salespeople can spend more time developing new customers.

EXERCISE: BUILD YOUR ACCOUNT PROFILE

Activities

- Select an account that you want to penetrate or grow.

- Research current data for the target account.

- Complete the Account Profile Template that follows.

Account Profile Template

Overview of the company

Description of its offerings

Analysis of its markets

Summary of its financial status

Description of its competition

Executive biographies, including descriptions of potential pains

Potential capabilities needed

The identification of key players and their pains from the Account Profile helps to create a picture of how each individual's pains are connected to others' in a cause-and-effect relationship. This takes us to our next basic principle.

PAIN FLOWS THROUGHOUT AN ENTIRE ORGANIZATION

Pain is felt by individuals, but the effects are broader and are felt throughout an entire organization. This is because organizations are highly interdependent. The activities, morale, and performance of one group affect the whole. One person's pain becomes the reason for another person's pain in an organization. In effect, if you resolve the pain of one person, then others benefit.

The challenges are first to recognize this business dynamic and second to identify how you can help the individuals involved. This cause-and-effect relationship is also called *organizational interdependency*.

IT Director
"I can't provide marketing data to the VP Marketing."

VP Marketing
"I can't develop effective campaigns to generate sales leads."

VP Sales
"I have a decline in sales revenue due to a lack of leads."

VP Finance
"My profitability is eroding as sales revenue declines."

The job aid that depicts organizational interdependency is called a Pain Chain. It is a picture of how pains flow throughout an organization.

Pain Chain

Overview
The Pain Chain is a graphical depiction of the cause-and-effect relationship of critical business issues (pains) inside an organization. It includes job title, pain, and the reasons for that pain.

Where/How Used
The Pain Chain is used in pre-call planning and research to better understand potential interdependencies in an opportunity.

In addition, after interviewing individuals to validate your assumptions, you can recraft your initial Pain Chain to reflect your new findings. Sharing this level of information with buyers during the sell cycle can help establish further credibility.

What You Should Achieve
A completed Pain Chain demonstrates to the buyer an insightful understanding of his or her business.

Input Required
To create a Pain Chain, you must understand the pains of key players in the organization and the reasons for their pains.

Pain Chain Example

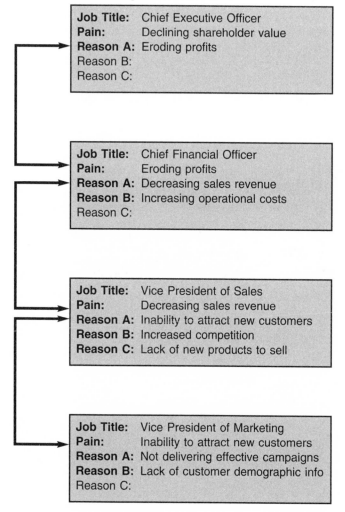

If you prepare a Pain Chain during the pre-call planning and research step, your job during the sell cycle is to verify and refine the information. A Pain Chain that has been completed prior to discussions with a prospective buyer is simply a stake in the ground that serves as a starting point for future conversations.

The illustration that follows shows a seven-step approach to building a Pain Chain.

How to Build a Pain Chain

Step 1 Target a job title as an entry point for the opportunity.

Step 2 List a high-priority pain for the job title targeted.

Step 3 Record reasons for the pain that your offering(s) can address.

Step 4 Ensure the pain becomes a reason for a different pain one level up.

Step 5 Ask, "What bad thing happens because of this reason?" The answer is the pain for a different key player.

Step 6 Ask, "Who is measured on this pain?" The answer will point to the different key player's job title.

Step 7 Repeat Steps 4 to 6 to drive the Pain Chain up another level to link to another key player.

Step 8 Connect key players down the chain by determining how reasons flow down to become pain.

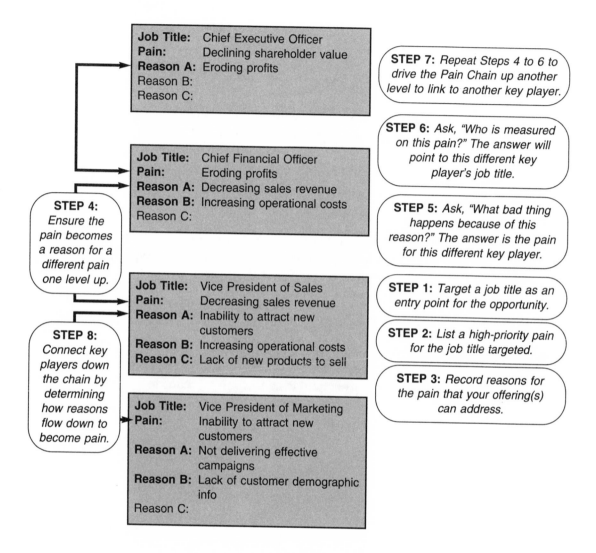

Once you have been able to craft an initial Pain Chain, you can begin to formulate a game plan that helps determine

- Which job title is the optimal person to attempt to stimulate interest with

- Whether that job title is a candidate to be a power sponsor

- What your business development strategy should be (i.e., the approach for stimulating interest with the targeted job title)

EXERCISE: BUILD YOUR PAIN CHAIN

Activities

- Identify the pain and its primary reason for a specific buyer (by job title) that you might encounter in a typical sales cycle. You should begin this activity by rezferring to one of the job titles and corresponding pains you recorded in "Exercise: Identify Potential Pains, Part I," found earlier in this chapter.

- Record the information in one of the blocks provided on the Pain Chain template.

- Trace the pain up and/or down the Pain Chain to include three other job titles in the buyer's organization that are affected by the pain.

- Refer to the section "How to Build a Pain Chain" for assistance.

Note: You may want to refer to the pain checklist introduced earlier in this chapter to ensure that you are accurately articulating the pains at each level of the Pain Chain.

Pain Chain Template

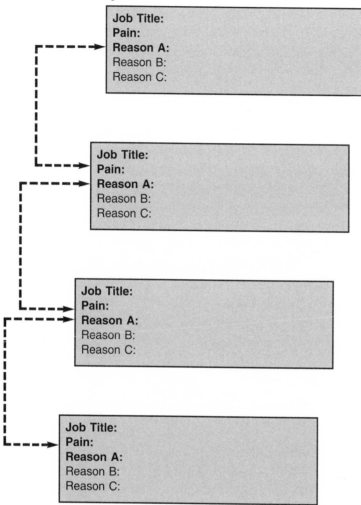

Summary

As mentioned at the beginning of this chapter, executing winning sales depends on the effectiveness of the planning and research that take place prior to making the call. My hope is that the exercises, job aids, and information sources concerning the identification of potential pains will inspire you to increase your own personal planning-to-executing ratio—and thereby improve your chances for sales success.

CHAPTER 4

HOW TO STIMULATE INTEREST WITH PROSPECTS

Why is stimulating interest with prospects important?

The ability to stimulate the interest of prospective buyers is the lifeblood of sales and marketing professionals. Those who can't master this ability will always find their sales pipeline wanting for more. As important as stimulating prospects' interest is to sustained success in business, it continues to be one of the most pressing challenges for everyone.

A survey commissioned by Sales Performance International and conducted by Equation Research polled sales professionals about the most critical job challenges they faced on a consistent basis. Over 50 percent of those surveyed said that "prospecting for new opportunities" was one of their top barriers to success.

Many sales professionals hate prospecting. They call it all sorts of different names—"business development," "interest creation," "demand generation"—because the mere mention of the word *prospecting* causes them to become uncomfortable.

People who find prospecting to be a challenge usually do so because of one of four factors:

1. *They don't properly define* prospecting *in the first place.* Prospecting should be viewed as *the ability to create and*

stimulate interest. Calling a buyer and asking, "Are you looking to buy what I'm selling?" isn't stimulating interest, it's polling.

2. *They forget "no pain, no change."* Their message doesn't target a potential pain of the prospect, but rather focuses on the selling organization's product or service.

3. *They create tension, not interest.* If their goal is simply to sell something instead of earning the right to have a conversation, distrust and discomfort arise for both parties.

4. *They have a fear of rejection.* Some rejection would go away if the salesperson simply avoided the three factors just mentioned. However, some rejection simply comes with the territory—not all prospects will be interested in your message or your offering.

In this chapter you'll find principles, exercises, and job aids that will help you deliver pain-oriented messages intended to create and stimulate interest. Those Solution Selling job aids are

| Business Development Prompters | Business Development Letters | Reference Stories | (Initial) Value Propositions |

Before starting to stimulate interest, it will be necessary to understand the different levels of need that buyers experience.

BASIC PRINCIPLE

THERE ARE THREE LEVELS OF BUYER NEED

You will find that buyers are at one of three different levels of need. By recognizing your buyer's level of need, you can determine the best tactics for developing the opportunity.

Level 1: latent pain The buyer is not actively attempting to address the pain and may even be unaware that a potential solution exists. Such a buyer may have failed at previous attempts to resolve the pain and therefore have rationalized that other solutions are too expensive, complicated, or risky. In other cases, the buyer may simply be unaware that there is a pain.

Level 2: admitted pain The buyer is willing to discuss pain, difficulty, or dissatisfaction with the existing situation. The buyer admits the pain but does not know how to address it.

Level 3: vision of a solution The buyer has admitted the pain, accepts responsibility for solving it, can visualize the details of a solution, and understands how the solution will address the pain.

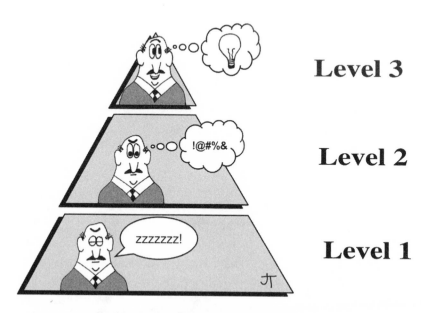

To stimulate your prospects' interest, you must incorporate pain into your messages. This chapter includes some useful job aids for doing this in an effective and consistent manner. Whether you use these job aids or create your own, consider whether your approach stands up to this business development checklist:

Business Development Checklist

Do your initial messages to prospects

- ❐ Take less than 30 seconds to deliver?

- ❐ Avoid sounding scripted and insincere?

- ❐ Target a pain that the prospect might have or be able to relate to?

- ❐ Imply that you have helped peers of the prospect resolve a potentially similar situation?

- ❐ Avoid a detailed description of your company history?

- ❐ Avoid in-depth descriptions of your products and/or services?

- ❐ Exclude asking the prospect to buy anything or to schedule a meeting?

- ❐ Avoid asking the prospect to admit an assumed pain?

To help you develop powerful messages that stimulate your prospects' interest, we recommend using the following Solution Selling job aids: the Business Development Prompter and a related letter or e-mail.

Business Development Prompter

Overview
A Business Development Prompter is a very brief, targeted script used to increase the success rate of stimulating interest.

Where/How Used

A Business Development Prompter is usually used to initiate contact over the telephone. The objective is to stimulate interest in order to motivate the prospect to want to learn about your products and services. The prompter can be modified for various approaches, but most versions should include these elements:

- Your name

- Your organization

- The targeted industry

- Number of years of experience within that industry

- A description of a pain experienced by others with a job title or role similar to that of the prospect and within the same or similar industry as the prospect

- A concise framework that allows the message to be delivered in under 30 seconds

What You Should Achieve

The purpose of using the Business Development Prompter is to have the prospect become curious enough to want to set up a future appointment or to ask to continue listening on the phone to learn how a peer has already solved a similar problem that she or he might have or can relate to.

Input Required

To build the Business Development Prompter, you will need knowledge of how you or your organization has helped other buyers (by title) solve pains within the targeted industry. Prior customer successes and Key Players Lists can be useful as input.

Note: The key elements of a Business Development Prompter for new prospects can also be modified to create variations of the prompter that emphasize a menu of pains approach, a customer referral approach, and so on. The key elements of a Business Development Prompter can also be used in written correspondence. See the discussion of Business Development Letters or e-mails that follows.

Business Development Prompter Examples

New Opportunity Option

This is Bill Hart *[salesperson's name]* with _____ *[name of sales organization]*. You and I haven't spoken before, but we have been working with manufacturing organizations *[target industry]* for the last 20 *[#]* years. One of the chief concerns we are hearing (lately) from other Sales Executives *[job title]* is their (frustration/difficulty) with missing revenue targets *[job title's likely pain]*.

We have been able to help our customers address this issue. Would you like to know how?

Menu of Pains Option

This is Bill Hart *[salesperson's name]* with _____ *[name of sales organization]*. You and I haven't spoken before, but we have been working with manufacturing organizations *[target industry]* for the last 20 *[#]* years. The top three (issues/concerns) we are hearing (lately) from other Sales Executives *[job title]* are:
(1) missing revenue targets,
(2) increasing cost of sales, and
(3) inability to accurately forecast sales revenue
            [job title's top three likely pains].

We have helped companies like: Warstler Toys, Universal Computers, and HandyMan Tools *[three reference organizations]* address some of these issues. Would you be curious in learning how?

Customer Referral Option

This is Bill Hart *[salesperson's name]* with _____ *[name of sales organization]*. You and I haven't spoken before, but Sandra Albertson, Vice President of Sales at Warstler Toys *[reference person's name, title, and organization]* suggested that I give you a call.

We were able to help (her/him) address (his/her) difficulty with missing revenue targets (due to an inappropriate level of customer service being attended to by her salespeople) *[reference person's pain]*. Would you be interested to know how?

Business Development Letter

Overview

The Business Development Letter is similar to the Business Development Prompter. It is a proactive letter or e-mail sent to stimulate interest and move a prospect from latent pain to admitted pain.

Where/How Used

The Business Development Letter is used to cold-mail prospects. The objective is to stimulate interest in order to motivate the prospect to want to learn about your products and services.

What You Should Achieve

The Business Development Letter should move the prospect from not looking to looking and should stimulate enough interest to have the prospect contact you or your organization for additional information. As part of your overall business development strategy, you may choose to send the Business Development Letter (e-mail) to a prospect and then follow it up with a call relating elements of the Business Development Prompter.

Input Required

To create a business development letter, you must have references and success stories of closed opportunities that information can be extracted from. The letter should contain the following elements:

- A benefit statement about your organization's core competency

- A statement highlighting your organization's experience in the targeted industry

- A description of multiple high-probability pains that the prospect may have

- Approved customer names to be used as references

Business Development Letter Example

Dear *Steve* [Prospect],

Our company is in the business of helping our customers achieve or surpass their revenue targets and control operational cost by greatly reducing the amount of time they spend on redundant and manual sales-related activities *[describe positioning statement using a "we help" theme]*.

We have been working with manufacturing *[industry]* companies for the last 20 *[#]* years.

Our clients include *[three reference organizations]*:
- (1) Warstler Toys,
- (2) Universal Computers, and
- (3) HandyMan Tools.

Some of the chief concerns we hear from them are *[top three potential pains]*:
- (1) missing revenue targets,
- (2) increasing cost of sales, and
- (3) inability to accurately forecast sales revenue.

We have been able to help our customers successfully deal with these and other issues. I would like an opportunity to share some examples with you. If you are interested in learning how we have helped other Vice Presidents of Sales *[job title]* solve some very challenging issues, please call me at 704-364-9298 *[phone number]* and I will provide you with more information.

Sincerely,
Bill Hart *[salesperson's name]*

EXERCISE: CREATE A BUSINESS DEVELOPMENT PROMPTER

Activities

- Use the Business Development Prompter templates that follow.

- Fill out each of the relevant Business Development Prompter templates with content that would be specific to a prospect whom you have yet to call on but would like to target during your prospecting activities.

- Use your work from "Exercise: Identify Potential Pains, Part I" (Chapter 3) to determine a job title and corresponding potential pain as the basis for filling out the prompter templates.

Business Development Prompter Templates

New Opportunity Option

This is _____ [your name] with _____
[your organization]. You and I haven't spoken before, but we have been working with _____ [target industry] for the last _____ [#] years. One of the chief concerns we are hearing (lately) from other _____ [job title] is their (frustration/difficulty) with _____ [job title's likely critical issue/pain].

We have been able to help our customers address this issue. Would you like to know how?

Menu of Pains Option

This is _____ [your name] with _____
[your organization]. You and I haven't spoken before, but we have been working with _____ [target industry] for the last _____ [#] years. The top three (issues/concerns) we are hearing (lately) from other _____ [job title] are:
(1) _____,
(2) _____, and
(3) _____
_____ [job title's top three likely critical business issues/pains].

We have helped companies like _____, _____, and _____ [three reference organizations] address some of these issues. Would you be curious in learning how?

Customer Referral Option:

This is _____ [your name] with _____
[your organization]. You and I haven't spoken before, but
_____, _____ at
_____ [reference person's name, title, and organization], suggested that I give you a call.

We were able to help (her/him) address (his/her) frustration/difficulty with
_____
[reference person's critical business issue/pain].
Would you be interested to know how?

EXERCISE: CREATE A BUSINESS DEVELOPMENT LETTER

Activities

- Use the Business Development Letter template that follows.

- Create a Business Development Letter that could be used in lieu of or in conjunction with the Business Development Prompter.

- Select one of the filled-out templates from "Exercise: Create a Business Development Prompter" earlier in this chapter as the basis for filling out the letter templates.

Business Development Letter Template

Dear _____ [prospect],

Our company is in the business of helping our customers _____
_____
[describe positioning statement using a "we help" theme].

We have been working with _____ [industry] companies for ___ [#] years.
Our clients include [three reference customer organizations]:

_____ ,

_____ , and

_____ .

Some of the chief concerns we hear from them are [top three potential
pains]:

_____ ,

_____ , and

_____ .

We have been able to help our customers successfully deal with these
and other issues. I would like an opportunity to share some examples with
you. If you are interested in learning how we have helped other
_____ [job title] solve some very challenging issues,
please call me at _____ [phone number] and I will provide
you with more information.

Sincerely,
_____ [salesperson's name]

Effective interest-stimulating messages focus on addressing pain, as indicated in the business development checklist. However, when pain messages are supported by a description of how you have helped peers of the prospect resolve a situation similar to the one the prospect faces—or at least one that the prospect can relate to—then the messages' strength greatly increases.

Give Pain to Get Pain

Imagine this: You are at a social gathering with your spouse or significant other, and you strike up a conversation with another couple that you have just met. The conversation naturally progresses to talking about families. They mention that their youngest child has had a lot of trouble at school lately. They tell you that their child has been late to class several times, has turned in homework assignments late, and has been reprimanded by teachers for talking out of turn.

If this couple shared this type of experience with you, what would be your likely natural response?

If you can relate at all to the couple's story, then you might respond by sharing a similar or worse experience. The natural reaction upon hearing a story like this is to respond with a story of your own.

Now, imagine how you would feel if a stranger approached you at the same party and asked, "So, do you have any problem children?"

At first this may sound silly, but in essence that is what salespeople are doing when they prematurely ask a prospective buyer to share pain with them. To earn the right to ask about pain, you have to give some pain. Sharing a customer reference story is an effective way to establish your credibility and offer pain to get pain.

Reference Story

Overview

The Reference Story is a job aid that provides you with a conversational prompter that helps you to stimulate interest, build credibility with a prospect, and get the prospect to admit pain. It gives you an opportunity to share a situationally specific story of how the prospect's peers have been helped by implementing capabilities provided by your organization.

Where/How Used
The Reference Story is used as a prompter, not a script. It is typically used as part of the stimulating interest step of the Solution Selling process, but it can be used effectively to assist in building credibility, getting pain admitted, and demonstrating proof at multiple stages in a sell cycle.

What You Should Achieve
When a Reference Story is used successfully,

- The prospect will feel comfortable enough to admit the pain.

- The prospect may divulge that she or he already has a vision of a solution.

- Enough credibility will be established that you will have earned the right to continue further conversation with the prospect.

Input Required
To create a Reference Story, you must have specific examples from previous successful opportunities and know the measurable results that were achieved.

Note: The ideal situation is to have a database of Reference Stories cataloged by the industries and job titles you are targeting. Additional Reference Stories should be added to the database as customers recognize results.

Reference Story Template and Format

Situation:	A customer job title and vertical industry
Pain:	The pain of the job title above
Reason(s):	One (or more) reasons for the pain, biased toward your product or service
Capabilities: *When, who, what:*	In the words of your customer, the business event, the player(s), and the specific capabilities needed to address the pain: "He/she/they said they needed a way to . . ."
We provided:	If the "solution" is described properly, all the person should have to state is, "We provided him/her/them with those capabilities."
Result:	Specific measurement is best (articulated in $ or %). The result should address the pain.

Reference Story Example

Situation:	VP Sales, manufacturing industry
Pain:	Missing new account revenue targets
Reason(s):	His customers were required to place all orders via their salesperson. Salespeople were spending all of their time servicing existing customers and not developing new ones.
Capabilities: *(when):* *(who):* *(what):*	He said they needed a way . . . When wanting to order, for existing customers to place their orders directly on the Internet, thus allowing his salespeople to have the time to develop new customers.
We provided:	"him with those capabilities."
Result:	Over the last six months, existing customers have placed 96 percent of all orders using the Internet. His salespeople have increased the size of the customer base 10 percent and overall revenue 6 percent.

When the Reference Story Might Be Used

1. *After delivering the message from a Business Development Prompter* After delivering your initial message, you next ask, "Would you like to know how?" Many prospects will indeed be curious and want to know more. They may even ask you about the client being referenced. This is a natural segue to describing the elements of the Reference Story in a conversational manner.

2. *As part of an introduction during a first call or meeting* I recommend that as part of your call objective, you state that you would like to tell the prospect about another customer you've worked with in the prospect's industry.

3. *To be used as a form of proof* Often prospective buyers will need some form of proof of your capabilities or value before they decide to make a purchase. Reference Stories can be shared with prospective buyers as a powerful yet inexpensive form of proof. This may lead naturally to an arranged call between your successful customer and the prospective buyer.

Reference Story Checklist

Does or is the Reference Story:

- ❏ Factual/true?
- ❏ Include measurable results?
- ❏ Concise and not a lengthy case study?
- ❏ Able to be told as a story, not plodded through as a worn-out script?
- ❏ Customer-focused, not "what I sold" focused?
- ❏ Avoid implying that you are accusing the prospect of having the exact same pain?
- ❏ Avoid divulging anything confidential without permission from the referenced customer?

Note: Review the current set of success stories or case studies that you or your organization are using and adapt them to the Solution Selling Reference Story format.

EXERCISE: CREATE A REFERENCE STORY

Scenario

When you share a Business Development Prompter or letter, prospects often want more detail about how you've helped a similar customer. You should be prepared to respond using the Reference Story format.

Activities

- Create a Reference Story using the template that follows.

- Link it to the situation you previously used in creating the Business Development Prompter and letters.

- Include results from a real customer success that are quantifiable and that address the cited pain.

Reference Story Template

Situation:	_____
Pain:	_____
	_____
Reason(s):	_____
	_____
Capabilities: _When, who, what:_	"He/she/they said they needed a way to . . ."
	_____
	_____
	_____
We provided:	"We provided him/her/them with those capabilities."
Result:	_____
	_____

Which one of the six elements associated with a Reference Story do you find most compelling?

The response to this question that I hear most often is results. Quantifiable results are compelling because they are what people want and what businesspeople demand.

While Reference Stories help stimulate interest, establish credibility, and provide a proof statement, there is another more aggressive Solution Selling job aid that you will want to consider: the Value Proposition.

Doesn't Everyone Have a Value Proposition?

In today's marketplace of overused phrases and marketing hype, many people roll their eyes or give an audible sigh when they hear the words *Value Proposition*. Value Proposition is a buzzword that has been used so often that it's lost its meaning for many of us.

The Solution Selling approach to Value Propositions is unique and when utilized properly can be an extremely powerful way to stimulate interest. There are three guidelines that must be followed when delivering Value Propositions to prospective buyers.

1. *The Value Proposition must not be a "Value-less" Value Proposition.* Value is best defined as benefits minus cost. So a real Value Proposition must suggest a quantifiable benefit to be gained as well as an estimate of the investment required by the prospective buyer.

2. *The Value Proposition should be customized.* Most so-called Value Propositions are not propositions of value, but rather tend to be statements of generic benefit. Your Value Proposition should be specific and should address a relevant pain of the person you are targeting or speaking to.

3. *The Value Proposition you deliver should be one you believe in.* If you don't believe in the value that can be delivered, then why should the prospective buyer?

 ## Value Proposition

Overview

A Value Proposition is a statement that *projects* the quantified value that a prospect should achieve through the use of your organization's capabilities. It is intended to stimulate interest and serve as the catalyst to begin an evaluation of your capabilities.

Where/How Used

Value Propositions can be used at any time or any place with a prospective buyer. They are most commonly used when you want to stimulate interest. After interest is stimulated, the Value Proposition serves as the basis point to work from with the prospect. After interest has been generated, the logical steps that follow should be to verify or revise the projections.

What You Should Achieve

The Value Proposition should help you stimulate a prospective buyer's interest and build credibility for you and your organization.

Input Required

To create a Value Proposition, you must have specific knowledge of the results and value already achieved by an existing customer. You will also need to know specific baseline information about the prospect you are targeting. Results found in customer Reference Stories provide a great source of data from which to extrapolate. Third-party sources such as OneSource provide good baseline metrics on the prospective buyer's business.

Value Proposition Template and Example

We believe that <u>Titan Games</u> *[prospect organization's name]*

should be able to <u>increase sales revenue</u>

[describe pain being addressed or area being improved]

by <u>10 percent</u> each year

(valued at <u>$10 million potential revenue or $3.2 million in profits annually</u>)

[how much in % and/or $]

through the ability to

<u>have customers place their own (repeat) orders, allowing salespeople</u>

<u>more business development time for new accounts</u>

[describe primary benefit]

as a result of <u>implementing our e-commerce offering</u>

[describe primary capability or enabler of offering/s]

for an approximate investment of <u>$1.15 million</u>

[prospect's relative investment $].

Value Proposition assumptions:
- Based on measured results of other clients, typically a 10 percent revenue increase occurs after implementing our e-commerce capabilities.
- One-time investment for this size organization is typically $1 million with an annual ongoing investment of $75,000.
- Research of TGI's gross profit margin (32 percent) and annual revenue ($100 million).

Although this Value Proposition example describes profits and investments in millions of dollars, a Value Proposition can and should be constructed for organizations of any size. The most important factor is that the potential benefits warrant the investment being asked for.

EXERCISE: PRACTICE CREATING A VALUE PROPOSITION

Note: Creating a Value Proposition based on a fictitious scenario will give you the opportunity to practice this skill prior to applying it to your own opportunity.

Activities

- Read the profile about the prospect organization, Second National Bank.
- Extrapolate the results from the successful customer, Third Charter Bank, to help develop a reasonable Value Proposition for Second National Bank.
- Read the profile for Third Charter Bank, including the assumptions made.
- Record any assumptions being made when developing the Value Proposition.
- Use the Value Proposition template that follows.

Successful Customer—Third Charter Bank

Your selling organization is in the business of providing online selling tools and prompters to your customers. You have successfully helped Third Charter Bank install an online menu of selling tools and prompters for its telemarketing channel.

- Third Charter's annual revenues are approximately $300 million, with 50 percent of that revenue coming from the retail banking group.
- The Executive Vice President of Retail Banking told you that his group needed the capability to view a particular

customer's account history while on the phone to prompt the telemarketers to up-sell and cross-sell, as well as provide customized scripting that would help the telemarketers carry the conversation through qualification and closing.

- The investment for these capabilities = $805,000:
  - Two servers and supporting equipment per call center ($80,000 × 2) = $160,000; @ 2 separate call centers = $320,000
  - Total software package (enterprise license) = $475,000
  - Implementation services = $1,000/day @ 5 days each per call center (× 2) = $10,000

- The result after six months of implementation is that the capabilities have helped the telemarketing channel to grow retail sales sixfold (1 percent hit rate grew to 6 percent). This resulted in an increase in overall retail sales of 10 percent or $15 million.

Profile: Prospect Organization—Second National Bank

Profile and Assumptions

Through pre-call planning and research, you believe that Second National Bank can greatly benefit from online menu and prompter capabilities.

- The current telemarketing hit rate is unknown.

- Second National's annual revenues are approximately $500 million, with 40 percent of that revenue coming from the retail banking group, as described in the company's annual report.

- The number of telemarketers employed by Second National is about the same as that for Third Charter, but they are all centrally located in one call center.

Value Proposition Template

We believe that <u>Second National Bank</u>

should be able to _____

[describe pain being addressed or area being improved]

by _____ [how much in % and/or $]

through the ability to _____

[describe primary benefit]

as a result of _____

[describe primary capability or enabler of offering/s]

for an approximate investment of _____

[prospect's relative investment $].

Value Proposition assumptions:
- Telemarketing hit rate will be the same.
-
-

<u>Answer</u>: We believe that Second National Bank should be able to _increase retail banking revenue_ by 10 percent or $20 million through the ability for your telemarketers _to better up-sell, cross-sell, and close qualified prospects and customers_ as a result of _implementing our online menu of selling tools and prompters_ for an approximate investment of _$640,000_. Assumptions: Telemarketing hit rate will be the same and the revenue increase will also be 10 percent.

EXERCISE: CREATE YOUR OWN VALUE PROPOSITION

Activities

- Use the Value Proposition Workspace that follows to brainstorm and develop your Value Proposition.

- Identify facts or key metrics from a successful customer that you feel are important in building your Value Proposition. This could include things like size, revenues, number of employees, profit margin, and so on. You probably used some of these when you built your Reference Story.

- Determine and record any assumptions being made.

- Extrapolate the results from your successful customer and project them upon the prospect organization.

- Use the Value Proposition template to document your Value Proposition.

Value Proposition Workspace

Successful Customer Facts

Initial Assumptions about Prospect Organization

Extrapolation

Value Proposition Template

We believe that _____ [prospect organization's name]

  should be able to _____

[describe the critical business issue being addressed or area being improved]

    by _____ [how much in % and/or $]

  through the ability to _____

[describe primary benefit]

  as a result of _____

[describe primary capability or enabler of offering/s]

  for an approximate investment of _____

[prospect's relative investment $].

Value Proposition assumptions:
■
■
■

Summary

The key to a good business development approach is not to focus on your products or services, but instead to focus on how your organization has helped to resolve pains that are similar to those faced by the prospective buyer.

If you find a prospect that isn't stimulated by your business development approach, remember the "SW" Rule:

> ***Some Will, Some Won't, So What? Someone Else Is Waiting!***

It's not personal. If someone is not interested in your message, then look for someone else who is interested.

CHAPTER 5

HOW TO HELP PROSPECTS ADMIT PAIN

How do you help prospects to admit pain?

Correctly identifying the pain that drives a sales opportunity is a critical element of successful selling. Fortunately, if a prospect's pain is acute, uncovering it is not that difficult. If you go to a doctor because of severe pain, you readily admit the pain and tell him or her as much as you can about the situation. When you are in pain, you want relief.

The challenge for salespeople occurs when prospective buyers are not in acute pain. Buyers who are in latent pain may not realize the severity of the situation, or they may have rationalized there is nothing they can do about it. In situations like this, getting prospective buyers to admit pain is difficult.

In Solution Selling, we've developed a structured sales call model to help you with this challenge. Instead of wandering through an unstructured sales call and conversation with a prospect, hoping that you'll develop enough rapport to get the prospect to trust you and admit pain, using a structured sales call model enables you to gain credibility and get the prospect to admit his or her pain.

The structured sales call approach

- Aligns "selling" steps with the decisions a prospect makes on a first call or the initial conversation with a salesperson.

- Establishes that the person leading the sales call or conversation is trustworthy and will add value.

- Allows the prospect to come to a self-admission of the pain.

In this chapter, you'll find principles, exercises, and job aids for a structured first call that leads prospects to admit their pain. The Solution Selling job aid that helps accomplish this is the

**Strategic Alignment Prompter
(Steps 1–3)**

Before we look specifically at the Strategic Alignment Prompter and its components, there are two basic principles that serve as the foundation of executing the steps of a structured call. Those basic principles are "people buy from people" and "power buys from power."

BASIC PRINCIPLE

PEOPLE BUY FROM PEOPLE

How would you respond if you were asked to complete this phrase: "People buy from people that they _____"? Like? Think are sincere? Believe are competent?

Those are important characteristics for buyers to see in salespeople—especially during a first call or an initial conversation.

However, you have to give your competitors the benefit of the doubt as also having those same characteristics. The distinguishing consideration is that people buy from people who *empower* them. Empowerment is the ability to allow a buyer to feel in control of the buying process.

The initial steps of the Strategic Alignment Prompter allow you to demonstrate that you are trustworthy

Trustworthiness = Sincerity + Competence

and are interested in empowering the prospect throughout the sell cycle.

The simple fact is that people buy from people. They don't buy from proposals, tenders, brochures, advertisements, or other such material. The prospect is looking for the salesperson to employ the real human element of selling by adding value to the exchange. The cartoon given here shows a sale that lacks the human element.

PERCEPTION EXERCISE
Question
Which of these figures would you label the "buyer" and which
the "salesperson"?

When I pose this question to groups of people, most will say
that the larger figure is the buyer and the smaller one is the
salesperson.

When I ask why, most answer that the larger figure has the
money. I won't argue that buyers are often in positions of power,
but I'm amazed at the number of salespeople who minimize the
power and value that they hold as well.

 BASIC
PRINCIPLE

POWER BUYS FROM POWER

People with power want to buy from people who also have
power. The term *power* is not synonymous with greed or arro-
gance; it's an internal confidence and external projection that
you should strive to possess. It implies to buyers, "I understand

your business issue, and I hope that we can work together to bring my resources to bear upon your situation for mutual benefit."

Power buys from power is a two-way street in which neither the buyer nor the salesperson loses power or takes power away from the other. Buyers prefer to buy from salespeople who have the most command over their company resources and demonstrate clout within their organization. Inversely, they prefer not to buy from salespeople who appear weak, use groveling phrases when they speak, and are not respectful of their own time and their company's resources.

Now that you have been introduced to two basic principles of a structured call, let's review the Strategic Alignment Prompter.

Strategic Alignment Prompter

Overview

The Strategic Alignment Prompter is a seven-step guide that helps you align your selling activities with the buying process, starting with a first call or initial conversation.

Where/How Used

The Strategic Alignment Prompter provides a framework that can be used to execute the activities of a first face-to-face meeting or first phone call. It should help you to identify when and how to

1. Establish rapport.

2. State the objective of the call and provide information that
   - Positions your organization.
   - Provides facts that allow the prospect to draw positive conclusions about you, your organization, and your offerings.
   - Shares a relevant Reference Story.

3. Lead the prospect to admit pain.

4. Develop the customer's needs.

5. Gain agreement to move forward.

6. Determine the prospect's ability to buy.

7. Either negotiate for access to power or qualify the buying and evaluation criteria with power.

What You Should Achieve

Successful alignment should initially provide you with an opportunity to demonstrate to a prospect that you are sincere and competent, thereby earning the right to continue exploring the prospect's situation. Continued alignment through the steps of the Strategic Alignment Prompter should result in the prospect's admitting pain and developing a vision of a solution that will resolve the pain, ending with a sense of mutual commitment between the salesperson and the prospect concerning the next steps.

Input Required

The Strategic Alignment Prompter, Steps 1 to 3, requires a call objective, a company positioning statement, company facts, and a Reference Story.

As I walk through the steps of the Strategic Alignment Prompter, in both this chapter and subsequent ones, there are a few important things you should keep in mind.

1. This is a "prompter" with sample text—not a Broadway stage script that you must follow verbatim.

2. This prompter assumes a scenario in which you will have a conversation with a prospect who doesn't know you, doesn't know much about your organization, and has not yet admitted pain. For situations that are not as stringent as this scenario, customize, scale, or eliminate the activities as necessary.

3. This prompter begins with the assumption that the prospect's interest has been stimulated.

STEP 1: ESTABLISH RAPPORT

Hundreds of books have been written on techniques for establishing rapport quickly. The irony is that rapport, by nature, is a relationship or bond that develops over time. Trying to compel prospects to like you as soon as possible is not very genuine or natural. Imagine a prospect's first impression of someone who acts ingenuous because he or she is trying to prematurely force rapport.

The best way to develop rapport is to consider the buyer's perspective, pay attention to the buyer's responses, and adapt your behavior to ensure alignment with the buyer's state of mind.

⇨ *What is the buyer's perspective during this step?*

The buyer is deciding whether he or she wants to listen to you at all. Recognize that the buyer may be friendly and seem attentive during a call, but still have made a decision to disengage. In other words, the buyer can be physically engaged but mentally disengaged.

⇦ *What are the activities that help you create alignment with the buyer at this step?*

Adopt a conservative approach that is genuine and courteous, states appreciation for the meeting, and does not force rapport.

Allow the prospect to set the tone of the meeting in order to determine if he or she wants to engage in further pleasantries—"small talk"—or seems ready to focus on "business talk."

STEP 2: CALL INTRODUCTION

⇨ *What is the buyer's perspective during this step?*

The buyer is trying to determine if you are different from other salespeople. Are you sufficiently trustworthy (sincere and competent) that the buyer will divulge information that is critical to moving forward?

⇦ *What are the activities that help you create alignment with the buyer at this step?*

If rapport has developed naturally during Step 1, and the prospect feels that you are sincere in wanting to help him or her solve a business problem, then the focus of Step 2 should be on demonstrating your competence. There are five activities that you should engage in during the call introduction that will serve to demonstrate your competence.

- State the call objective.
- Share a positioning statement.
- Provide a company and personal introduction.
- Share a relevant Reference Story.
- Transition to getting pain admitted.

☐ STATE THE CALL OBJECTIVE

State the call objective and set a proposed agenda for the meeting. This indicates that you have a purpose. If the prospect has something else in mind, then you want to know that, too. Conclude the call objective with a statement that you are not going to try to continue "selling" to the prospect if there is no mutual benefit. This gives the prospect an "out," gives him or her a sense of being in control, and helps to reduce any discomfort he or she may be feeling.

> *"What I would like to do today is to introduce you to my company and tell you about another ___ (title and industry) we have worked with. I would then like to learn about you and your situation. At that point, the two of us will be able to make a mutual decision as to whether or not we should proceed any further."*

❏ SHARE A POSITIONING STATEMENT

Here you are making a high-level statement about how you help customers. The message should be tailored to be specific to the job title, role, and potential pain of the person that you are talking to.

> *"My company is in the business of helping organizations in the manufacturing industry achieve or surpass their revenue targets and control operational cost by greatly reducing the amount of time spent on redundant and manual sales-related activities."*

❏ PROVIDE A COMPANY AND PERSONAL INTRODUCTION

The point of providing a company and personal introduction is to share relevant facts that are intended to help the prospect draw desirable conclusions about you and your organization. It is not intended to be a cumbersome list of marketing claims.

"Just to tell you a little more about my organization and myself, we've been helping manufacturing organizations for over 25 years now. We have worked with 50 of the Fortune 500 companies. I personally have been with my company for the last 20 years . . ."

☐ SHARE A RELEVANT REFERENCE STORY

At this point, you want to get the prospect to start talking about his or her pain. The goal has been to establish credibility so that the prospect will feel comfortable sharing this pain. Here is where you can "share pain to get pain." It is useful to relate a Reference Story describing how a peer of the prospect (with the same or similar job responsibility in a similar industry) had a problem and solved it with your help. Use a Reference Story that you prepared or selected during pre-call planning and research.

"A particular situation you might be interested in is another manufacturing organization. Their Vice President of Sales and Marketing was having difficulty achieving his new account revenue targets. The reasons for his difficulty were____. He said he needed a way to____. We provided him with____. As a result, his customer base increased by 10 percent and overall revenue by 6 percent.

☐ MAKE THE TRANSITION TO GETTING PAIN ADMITTED

At this point, you should have accomplished your role within the agreed-upon call objective. You have introduced yourself and your organization to the prospect, and you have told the prospect about a person with a similar job title in a similar industry to the prospect's that your organization has worked with. Now, it is time to turn ownership of the conversation over to the prospect by saying, "But enough about how we helped another organization, tell me about you and your situation."

Here you invite the prospect to react to the Reference Story.

Before exploring the potential responses a buyer might have to a Reference Story, practice applying the call introduction elements to your own opportunity.

EXERCISE: DEVELOP YOUR CALL INTRODUCTION, PART I

Activities

- Identify your prospect by job title and industry. (*Note:* You may have already identified the prospect if the business development job aids created in the previous chapter stimulated the prospect's interest.)

- Create your call objective by filling in the blanks in the worksheet that follows or modifying the example to suit your situation.

- Create your positioning statement, incorporating a "we help" theme, in the space provided on the worksheet.

Call Introduction Worksheet, Part 1

Prospect: Job title: _____, industry: _____

Step 2: Call Introduction

☐ State the call objective

"What I would like to do today (*or* during the next _____ minutes) is to
- Introduce you to _____ *[your company name]* and
- Tell you about another _____ *[job title]* in the _____ industry *[specific industry]* we have worked with.
- I would then like to learn about you and your situation.
- Then the two of us will be able to make a mutual decision as to whether or not we should proceed any further."

☐ Share a positioning statement

"*[Your company name]* is in the business of helping organizations in the _____ industry *[specific industry]* _____
_____
_____."

EXERCISE: DEVELOP YOUR CALL INTRODUCTION, PART II

Activities

- Provide a company and personal introduction.

- List five examples of things you would want the prospective buyer to conclude about you and your selling organization.

- Use the worksheet that follows to record your conclusions in the left-hand column.

Call Introduction Worksheet, Part 2

	CONCLUSIONS		
1		⇔	
2		⇔	
3		⇔	
4		⇔	
5		⇔	

EXERCISE: DEVELOP YOUR CALL INTRODUCTION, PART III

Activities

- Check your list of conclusions. Are any of them facts? Or are they primarily opinions?

- Read through your list of conclusions again. Now, put yourself in the shoes of the prospect. How does the list sound? Is it compelling or not? If not, then do the following:
  - At the top of the right-hand column, label the header "FACTS." For each of the conclusions, record a fact that might help the prospect or buyer draw that desired conclusion.
  - Then select a few of the compelling facts and read them aloud. Again, put yourself in the prospect's shoes. How does the list sound? More compelling or not?

It is important that you provide only facts, not opinions, early in the sales call, because you have not yet established enough credibility with the prospect. Until you do, your opinion probably means little to the prospect.

Potential Responses to the Reference Story

Picking up where we left off before the exercises, I suggested that you could make the transition to getting pain admitted by reading a Reference Story and inviting a reaction by saying: "But enough about how we helped another organization, tell me about you and your situation."

Generally, any response you get from the prospect will fall into one of five categories. You are at a stage in the call where the buyer's response is going to greatly dictate your selling activities.

Five Potential Responses to a Reference Story

1. "I'm having that same problem" (as mentioned in the Reference Story).

2. "I'm having a different problem." (Not the same pain, but because your credibility is high, the prospect will share the pain with you.)

3. No pain is admitted; still, the prospect is friendly and talkative. (This is not a bad situation, but the conversation needs to become focused around a potential pain that you can address.)

4. No pain is admitted, and the prospect is *not* friendly and talkative. (This is not a good situation, but before disengaging, offer some potential pains that the prospect might relate to.)

5. "I have that same problem, and we're already working on it." (Is this a good or a bad situation? It is an active opportunity; the prospect already has a vision of a solution, and you are late in addressing the opportunity!)

Five Corresponding Actions to Take

1. "I'm having that same problem." Diagnose the problem and *create a vision*.

2. "I'm having a different problem." Diagnose the problem and *create a vision*.

3. No pain or problem is admitted; still, the prospect is friendly and talkative. *Ask situation questions* to help direct the conversation toward pain.

4. No pain is admitted, and the prospect is *not* friendly and talkative. *Ask a "menu of pain" question*.

5. "I have that same problem, and we're already working on it." *Reengineer the vision*.

Responses 1 and 2 require the skill of creating a vision of your solution. In Chapter 6, I will discuss vision creation in detail. Response 5 requires the skill of reengineering a buyer's existing vision. In Chapter 8, I will discuss vision reengineering.

In Responses 3 and 4, pain has not been admitted.

STEP 3: GET PAIN ADMITTED

⇨ *What is the buyer's perspective during this step?*

The buyer is trying to determine if he or she wants to admit the pain.

⇨ *What are the activities that help you create alignment with the buyer at this step?*

In Response 3, the prospect is friendly and talkative, but has not admitted pain. It is time to ask situation questions.

In Response 4, the prospect is neither friendly nor talkative. His or her time and patience may be limited. Pose a question offering a menu of pain.

Situation Questions

Situation questions can help funnel responses from a prospect down to either admitting the pain or providing information that can help you to anticipate the pain. Situation questions tend to be open questions in the sense that they allow the prospect to answer in any manner he or she chooses. They invite the prospect to engage in further conversation. Remember the basic principle: *No pain, no change*. We are trying to get the conversation focused on pain.

Examples of Situation Questions

"Today, when your customers want to place an order on a day their salesperson is not going to call them, what do they do?"

"Today, how do your customers get notified of new products or promotions?"

"When a prospect calls a salesperson to ask a FAQ, how is that call handled?"

"How do your salespeople get referrals from existing customers today?"

Menu of Pain Question

If pain is still not admitted and it appears that the conversation is going nowhere, it may be time to ask more direct questions. This is where a menu of pain approach may prove useful. A menu of pain question tends to be a closed question that elicits a yes or no response.

Example of a Menu of Pain Question

"The top three difficulties we are hearing from Vice Presidents of Sales these days are

1. Missing revenue targets,

2. Increasing cost of sales, and

3. Inability to accurately forecast sales revenue.

Are you facing any of these issues today?"
   or
Are you curious how we have helped our customers deal with these issues?"

EXERCISE: DEVELOP SITUATION AND MENU OF PAIN QUESTIONS

Activities

- Using the worksheet that follows, develop a series of situation questions that you believe would lead your prospect to admit pain.

- Develop a menu of pain question that can be used if the same prospect is less friendly and less talkative.

Situation Questions:
■
■
■
■
■

Menu of Pain Questions:

"The top three difficulties we are hearing from _____ *[job title]* these days are

1. _____

2. _____

3. _____

Are you facing any of these issues today?" *or*
Are you curious how we have helped our customers deal with these issues?"

In this chapter, we looked at the first three steps of the Strategic Alignment Prompter. The guide that follows shows those three steps collectively and highlights the key points. I encourage you to use this guide as a framework and planning worksheet prior to making first calls.

Strategic Alignment Prompter (Steps 1 through 3): Call Preparation Guide

Step 1: Establish Rapport

☐ **Let the prospect set the tone of the meeting**

> "I appreciate the opportunity to meet with you."
> Read the need for "small talk" or "business talk."

> *Avoid actions that may be perceived as insincere.*

Step 2: Introduce Call

☐ **State the call objective**

"What I would like to do today (*or* during the next _____ minutes) is to
- Introduce you to _____ *[your company name]* and
- Tell you about another _____ *[job title]* in the _____ industry *[specific industry]* we have worked with.
- I would then like to learn about you and your situation.
- Then the two of us will be able to make a mutual decision as to whether or not we should proceed any further."

> *State an objective at the beginning of all meetings.*

> *Let the prospect know that he or she has an "out."*

☐ **Share a positioning statement (use "we help" theme)**

"*[Your company name]* is in the business of helping organizations in the _____ industry *[specific industry]* _____
_____
_____."

> *Create a customized statement with the prospect in mind.*

☐ **Provide a company and personal introduction**

Conclusions		Facts
	⇔	
	⇔	
	⇔	

> *Determine what you want the prospect to conclude.*

☐ **Share a relevant Reference Story or progress-to-date anecdote**

"A particular situation you might be interested in is another _____ *[organization type]*. Its _____ *[job title]* was having difficulty with _____ *[pain]*. The reasons for his/her difficulty were _____. What he/she said was needed was a way to _____. We provided him/her with those capabilities. And the result was _____."

> *Ensure that your Reference Stories are pain-focused, not product-focused.*

☐ **Make the transition to getting pain admitted**

"But enough about *[how we helped another organization]*. Tell me about you and your situation."

Step 3: Get Pain Admitted

If pain has not been admitted:
- But the buyer is talking freely → ask situation questions.
- And the buyer is not talking freely → ask pain or menu of pain questions.

Once pain is admitted, prioritize it.

> *Prepare questions that help lead the buyer to admitting pain.*

Summary

Correctly identifying the pain that drives a sales opportunity is a critical element of successful selling. Sharing the pains of peers is a useful and effective technique to get your prospects to admit their own pains.

CHAPTER 6

HOW TO DIAGNOSE PAIN AND CREATE A VISION OF A SOLUTION

Why is diagnosing buyers' pain and creating a vision of a solution important?

The primary reason is based upon a Solution Selling principle—no pain, no change. In other words, without pain, buyers are not going to take action and change. And secondarily, if they do have pain and want to change, what action to take is the critical question. This is why creating a vision is so important. It's hard for buyers to take action without first having a vision of *what* to do. The salesperson who diagnoses pain and creates the vision of a solution most often wins the business.

A sales professional who doesn't first diagnose the buyer's pain and then help the buyer to visualize how his or her company's capabilities are going to help unwittingly puts him- or herself in the position of being just another salesperson. This type of salesperson brings little or no value to the prospective buyer or the capabilities he or she represents.

When a salesperson skips or minimizes the diagnosis of buyer pain,

- Both the buyer and the salesperson may remain blind to the depth of the pain and the reasons for it.

- The buyer may not be convinced that the salesperson fully understands his business.

- The salesperson may assume too much and be wrong.

When a salesperson skips or minimizes the creation of a vision of a solution:

- The salesperson may incorrectly assume that the buyer completely understands how his or her company's capabilities will address the pain.

- The salesperson misses an opportunity to set proper expectations.

In this chapter, you'll find principles, exercises, and job aids that help you to thoroughly diagnose a buyer's pain and then create a vision of a solution that is biased toward your offerings. Those Solution Selling job aids are

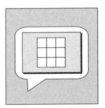

**9 Block Vision Processing Model—
Vision Creation**

Pain Sheet

EXERCISE: ANALYZE TWO SCENARIOS

Activity
Read these two scenarios and answer the three questions that follow.

Scenario A
You become ill while out of town and decide to visit an urgent care physician. You sit in the waiting room for over an hour before a nurse conducts the mandatory reading of your temperature, blood pressure, and weight. After another 20 minutes of waiting, you finally see the physician. She asks, "So what seems

to be the problem?" You reply, "Well, I've had a headache, sore throat, sniffles, and a high fever for several days." To that, the physician immediately replies, "I know just what you need!" and ends the appointment by writing a prescription.

Scenario B
You become ill while out of town and decide to visit an urgent care physician. You sit in the waiting room for over an hour before a nurse conducts the mandatory reading of your temperature, blood pressure, and weight. After another 20 minutes of waiting, you finally see the physician. He asks, "So what seems to be the problem?" You reply, "Well, I've had a headache, sore throat, sniffles, and a high fever for several days." The physician then asks several questions, such as, "How many days have you felt this way? Have you been in contact with anyone else who has been sick? Have you traveled outside of this region in the last few weeks? Do you have any allergic reactions to food?" After listening to your answers, the physician then checks your ears, nose, and throat and listens to your breathing with a stethoscope. Upon completion of the examination, the physician says, "The bad news is that you have influenza. The good news is that I am working with several other patients with the same thing, and with rest and a specific medication, you'll be fine." The appointment ends with the physician writing a prescription.

Two Questions about the Two Scenarios
1. Which scenario made you feel more comfortable?

    _____

2. What was the major difference between the two scenarios?

    _____

When I pose these two scenarios and questions to participants in Solution Selling workshops, almost all of them answer the question, "Which scenario made you feel more comfortable?" by answering "Scenario B."

When asked the next question, "What was the major difference between the two scenarios?" the overwhelming response is the approach being used by the physician. In the second scenario, the approach was much more consultative and made you trust the physician and the prescription much more.

In both scenarios, the physician probably knew the "answer" upon hearing the initial symptoms. However, keep in mind that if you don't trust the diagnosis, you won't trust the prescription.

> # DIAGNOSE BEFORE YOU PRESCRIBE

The key is to do a good job *diagnosing* your buyer's pain. If buyers don't trust your diagnosis, they won't trust your prescription. The cartoon that follows depicts a salesperson guilty of prescribing prematurely.

So how does a salesperson diagnose before prescribing? It's a matter of asking the right questions at the right time.

The 9 Block Vision Processing Model is a diagnostic questioning model that serves as a road map for having consultative conversations with buyers. Much like devices used to regulate the speed of some engines, the 9 Block Vision Processing Model helps to regulate the speed of its user so that he or she is prompted to thoroughly diagnose before prescribing.

Building the 9 Block Vision Processing Model

The intent of this chapter is primarily to help you develop the most effective questions to thoroughly diagnose your buyer's pain and then create a vision of a solution that is biased toward your capabilities.

The next several pages include content and exercises to explain the key elements of the model. If you are already very familiar with the 9 Block Vision Processing Model and would like to skip ahead to the application portion of this chapter, you should go to the section "How to Build a Pain Sheet."

 9 Block Vision Processing Model for Vision Creation

Overview

The 9 Block Vision Processing Model for Vision Creation is a buyer-focused questioning model used to diagnose an admitted pain and lead the buyer through self-conclusion to a vision of a solution.

Where/How Used

The framework of the 9 Block Vision Processing Model is derived by employing three types of questions:

- Open questions

- Control questions

- Confirming questions

These questions are used to cover three significant areas of exploration:

- Diagnosis of reasons for pain

- Exploration of the impact of pain on others

- Help in visualizing the capabilities needed

The 9 Block Vision Processing Model for Vision Creation is used (when latent pain opportunities exist.) You would navigate the model in a suggested sequence, leading the buyer to a buying vision.

Note: For active opportunities, you must reengineer a buyer's existing vision. This is done using the same model, but navigated in a different sequence. See Chapter 8, "How to Reengineer a Vision of a Solution."

What You Should Achieve

A successful use of the 9 Block Vision Processing Model for Vision Creation should result in the prospective buyer developing a buying vision of how to address an admitted pain utilizing your capabilities. Both you and the buyer should have a clearer appreciation of the measurable value associated with resolving the buyer's pain. Also, both of you should have an understanding of the impact that the pain has across the buyer's organization.

Input Required

Pain Sheets are situationally specific job aids that help prompt a salesperson to ask intelligent, control-oriented questions in the control row of the 9 Block Vision Processing Model.

Question Types of the 9 Block Vision Processing Model

Three types of questions are used in the 9 Block Vision Processing Model, as follows:

Open questions Open-ended questions invite buyers to talk freely, respond from experience, knowledge, and points of concern, and earn you the right to ask control questions. They are comfortable questions for buyers to answer because they are typically perceived as nonthreatening. They do have one disadvantage: They give control of the conversation to the buyer. That's not good if the direction the buyer takes has nothing to do with your offering. But early in the buying process, it's important for buyers to feel comfortable, so you are best advised to start with open questions.

CONTROL

Control questions Control questions are similar to closed or closed-ended questions. I prefer to use the term *control question* because it better describes the approach. Closed questions tend to be answered with a yes or no, whereas control questions tend to elicit more complete responses. Control questions also help to elicit quantitative information about things, such as "how much?" or "how often?" Control questions seek specific pieces of information, and help guide the buyer in the specific direction you want her or him to go.

CONFIRM

Confirming questions Confirming questions ensure that both the buyer and the salesperson are in sync. Confirming questions help summarize your understanding of the buyer's responses and demonstrate an ability to listen, show empathy, and exhibit expertise. Confirming questions can also help rectify any misunderstanding that may have occurred during a conversation.

EXERCISE: BUILDING THE 9 BLOCK MODEL, PART I

Activities

- Test your recognition of open, control, and confirming questions:
  - Read the list of questions that follows.
  - Determine which type of question each sample question is: an open, control, or confirming question.
  - Record your answers in the right-hand column of the worksheet labeled "Type."

	Question	Type
1.	Do you think one reason you missed your profit targets is because the financial reports were late?	
2.	So, what do you feel is the most significant factor in your recent decline in customer satisfaction?	
3.	How is system downtime having an effect on your sales and marketing efforts?	
4.	Would it help you if, when you needed reports, any of your team members could access, sort, and print them from one location?	
5.	You indicated that a lack of product research was causing you to keep from growing your market share, is that correct?	
6.	What have you tried to do to resolve the increasing number of late shipments to customers?	
7.	How often does that situation occur?	
8.	So if you had the 24/7 service we discussed, do you think that would help you increase your customer base?	
9.	Have you tried to resolve the increasing number of late shipments to customers?	
10.	From what I just heard you say, it sounds like this is not just a departmental issue but a company one?	
11.	Who else is concerned about this issue?	
12.	So, you have tried to resolve the increasing number of late shipments to customers?	
13.	Are the shrinking margins causing the value of your company's stock to decline?	
14.	How do you see yourself using our software and service offering within your organization?	
15.	It sounds like you want customers to be able to place orders online in order to minimize inventory; is that accurate?	

Answers: 1, 4, 7, 9, 13 = control; 2, 3, 6, 11, 14 = open; 5, 8, 10, 12, 15 = confirm.

Areas of Exploration in the 9 Block Vision Processing Model

Through the use of open, control, and confirming questions, the 9 Block Vision Processing Model guides the dialogue with a *Purpose* buyer in exploring three important aspects of understanding and (i) addressing the buyer's pain, as follows:

DIAGNOSE REASONS	*EXPLORE IMPACT*	*VISUALIZE CAPABILITIES*
You attempt to explore and understand all of the contributing factors associated with why the buyer is experiencing the admitted pain. Additionally, you want to diagnose how much, from a quantitative perspective, each reason is contributing to the buyer's pain.	After diagnosing the reasons for pain, you attempt to explore the impact that the buyer's pain has on other customer individuals. The intent is to see how pervasive the pain is throughout the organization. This dialogue can serve to verify, modify, or construct a Pain Chain.	After having diagnosed the reasons for pain and the other people affected, you must now attempt to help the buyer visualize a solution. In a consultative manner, you should vividly describe an action vision of how your capabilities might help the buyer address the reasons for the pain.

EXERCISE: BUILDING THE 9 BLOCK MODEL, PART II

Activities

- Test your recognition of the three areas of exploration:
  - Read the list of questions that follows.
  - Determine whether each sample question is an example of "diagnosing reasons," "exploring impact," or "visualizing capabilities."
  - Record your answers in the right-hand column labeled "Area to Explore."

Question	Area to Explore
1. Do you think one reason you missed your profit targets is because the financial reports were late?	
2. So, what do you feel is the most significant factor in your recent decline in customer satisfaction?	
3. How is system downtime having an effect on your sales and marketing efforts?	
4. Would it help you if, when you needed reports, any of your team members could access, sort, and print them from one location?	
5. You indicated that a lack of product research was causing you to keep from growing your market share, is that correct?	
6. What have you tried to do to resolve the increasing number of late shipments to customers?	
7. How much does that contribute to your problem?	
8. So if you had the 24/7 service we discussed, you think that would help you increase your customer base?	
9. Have you tried to resolve the increasing number of late shipments to customers?	
10. From what I just heard you say, it sounds like this is not just a departmental issue but a company one?	
11. Who else is concerned about this issue?	
12. So, you have tried to resolve the increasing number of late shipments to customers?	
13. Are the shrinking margins causing the value of your company's stock to decline?	
14. How do you see yourself using our software and service offering within your organization?	
15. It sounds like you want customers to be able to place orders online in order to minimize inventory; is that accurate?	

Answers: 1, 2, 7, 9, 10, 12 = diagnosing reasons; 3, 5, 11, 13 = exploring impact; 4, 6, 8, 14, 15 = visualizing capabilities.

When you combine the three types of question and the three areas of exploration, you naturally develop a questioning matrix with nine sections. This is the framework of the 9 Block Vision Processing Model.

	DIAGNOSE REASONS	EXPLORE IMPACT	VISUALIZE CAPABILITIES
OPEN			
CONTROL			
CONFIRM			

EXERCISE: BUILDING THE 9 BLOCK MODEL, PART III

Activities

- Determine the optimal sequence for navigating the 9 Block Vision Processing Model:
  - Read and answer the seven true-false questions that follow.

1.	You tend to have a more effective conversation with a buyer when you ask open questions *before* asking control questions.	True False
2.	Confirming questions should be the *first* type of question that you ask a buyer.	True False
3.	You should explore impact *before* helping a buyer to visualize how your capabilities might help.	True False
4.	You should explore impact *before* diagnosing the reasons for a buyer's admitted pain.	True False
5.	Open questions should be asked *after* control questions so that you can maintain as much control as possible during the conversation.	True False
6.	You should diagnose reasons *before* helping a buyer to visualize how your capabilities might help.	True False
7.	You should ask confirming questions *after* each of the areas of exploration to clarify the information gathered from asking open and control questions.	True False

Answers:
1. True. Psychologically speaking, buyers feel more comfortable when they have answered an open-ended question and therefore will allow you to ask control-oriented questions.
2. False. There is nothing to confirm if dialogue with the buyer has not taken place.
3. True. Remember "diagnose before you prescribe"; exploring the impact is still considered diagnosis. Helping the buyer to visualize capabilities leans toward the prescription.
4. False. Although impact questions are very important, you should focus on diagnosing the reasons for pain first. Once credibility has been demonstrated, the buyer will be more willing to allow dialogue that extends to discussing the impact of pain on others.
5. False. As answered in Question 1, buyers tend to feel more comfortable when they have answered an open-ended question prior to answering control-oriented questions.
6. True. Diagnose before you prescribe.
7. True. Although confirming questions can be asked at any time in a conversation, they can be most effective in confirming information uncovered during one area of exploration prior to beginning the next area of exploration.

If you answered all of the questions correctly (or at least agree with the answers), then you should have determined the optimal sequence for navigating the 9 Block Vision Processing Model, as depicted in the following graphic:

	DIAGNOSE REASONS	EXPLORE IMPACT	VISUALIZE CAPABILITIES
OPEN	(1)	(4)	(7)
CONTROL	(2)	(5)	(8)
CONFIRM	(3)	(6)	(9)

The 9 Block Vision Processing Model is a framework and prompter that helps people have meaningful conversations with buyers. As a result, I provide suggested text within the blocks of the model that serves as prompting words. This text has been used (and proven effective) by thousands of salespeople and sales support people throughout the years. However, I do encourage users to take the model and wrap their own words around it. The next exercise should help you place sample text in its appropriate block.

EXERCISE: BUILDING THE 9 BLOCK MODEL, PART IV

Activities

- Read the list of nine questions that follows.

- Draw a line connecting each question to the appropriate numbered box as it might be found within the 9 Block Vision Processing Model for Vision Creation.

QUESTIONS

Open Question Diagnose Reasons — 1	"So, the main reasons for your [*pain*] are . . . ?"
Control Question Diagnose Reasons — 2	"Would it help if you had the ability to . . . ?"
Confirming Question Diagnose Reasons — 3	"From what I heard, this [*pain*] affects others in your company, such as . . . ?"
Open Question Explore Impact — 4	"Tell me about it: What is causing you to have this [*pain*]?"
Control Question Explore Impact — 5	"So, if you had all those capabilities, then you could resolve your [*pain*]?"
Confirming Question Explore Impact — 6	"What is it going to take for you to be able to resolve this [*pain*]?"
Open Question Visualize Capabilities — 7	"Is one reason for your [*pain*] . . . ?"
Control Question Visualize Capabilities — 8	"Is this [*pain*] causing . . . [*increased operational cost*]?"
Confirming Question Visualize Capabilities — 9	"Who else is affected by this [*pain*] and how are they affected?"

Answers:
1 - "Tell me about it: What is causing you to have this [*pain*]?"
2 - "Is one reason for your [*pain*] . . . ?"
3 - "So, the main reasons for your [*pain*] are . . . ?"
4 - "Who else is affected by this [*pain*] and how are they affected?"
5 - "Is this [*pain*] causing . . . [*increased operational cost*]?"
6 - "From what I heard, this [*pain*] affects others in your company, such as . . . ?"
7 - "What is it going to take for you to be able to resolve this [*pain*]?"
8 - "Would it help if you had the ability to . . . ?"
9 - "So, if you had all those capabilities, then you could resolve your [*pain*]?"

When you include the sample text within the 9 Block Vision Processing Model for Vision Creation, the model provides a useful diagnostic tool for prompting you to ask consultative questions intended to guide a buyer from admitted pain to a buying vision.

PAIN

	DIAGNOSE REASONS	EXPLORE IMPACT	VISUALIZE CAPABILITIES
OPEN	R1 (1) "Tell me about it, what is causing you to have this... (repeat pain)?"	I1 (4) "Besides yourself, WHO in your organization is impacted by this (pain) and HOW are they impacted?"	C1 (7) "What is it going to take for YOU to be able to (achieve your goal)?" "Could I try a few ideas on you?"
CONTROL	R2 (2) "Is it because...?"	I2 (5) "Is this (pain) causing...?" "If so, would (title) also be concerned?"	C2 (8) "You mentioned (repeat reason) ...What if there were a way... *when, who, what* So that... ? ...would that help?
CONFIRM	R3 (3) "So, the reasons for your (repeat pain) are...? Is that correct?"	I3 (6) "From what I just heard... (repeat the WHO and HOW), it sounds like this is not just your problem, but a _____ problem! Is that correct?"	C3 (9) "So, IF you had the ability to (summarize capability visions), THEN could you (*achieve your goal*)?"

BUYING VISION

 If you engage in smaller situations or transactional sales, you may decide to use a streamlined version of the 9 Block Vision Processing Model. You may find it appropriate to skip both the impact column and the confirming questions. The 9 Block Model becomes a 4-Block Model for simpler sales transactions.

When people in sales and marketing roles review the 9 Block Vision Processing Model for the first time, they tend to have several common reactions:

- The model's composition is straightforward and practical.
- The open-ended questions are very easy to ask.

- The confirming questions are relatively easy to ask as long as the user takes notes during the dialogue with the buyer and has listened attentively.

- The control questions (the middle row of the 9 Block Vision Processing Model) are the most significant questions to ask because they elicit important buyer information. As a result, the control questions require the most thought and preparation.

Control questions are indeed the most significant questions in the model. That's why I recommend a tool or a job aid that helps identify, document, and facilitate how to ask these important questions. This job aid is called a Pain Sheet. The Pain Sheet is a useful tool that can be leveraged over and over by multiple people for different opportunities.

Pain Sheet

Overview

A Pain Sheet is a questioning prompter used with the 9 Block Vision Processing Model. It provides a set of control questions to help diagnose the reasons for a buyer's pain, identify the impacts of that pain on the rest of the organization, and describe the capabilities that could be provided to address the reasons for the pain. It is an integral job aid for creating (or reengineering) visions biased toward specific offerings or solutions of the selling organization.

Where/How Used

The Pain Sheet is used with the 9 Block Vision Processing Model to assist in asking questions that help you to create (or reengineer) a customer buying vision that is biased toward your specific offerings. The Pain Sheet can be used during conversations with buyers or prior to a meeting as a pre-call preparation aid.

What You Should Achieve

Asking the questions on a Pain Sheet should help you to

- Uncover reasons for the buyer's pain while biasing those reasons toward your offering.

- Determine the quantifiable value of addressing the reasons by asking "drill-down" questions (also found on the Pain Sheet).

- Develop a view (or modify an existing view) of how the buyer's pain affects others throughout his or her organization (Pain Chain).

- Position your capabilities in a manner that clearly helps the buyer visualize how and what he or she will be able to do differently in the future.

Input Required

To build a Pain Sheet, you will need an understanding of the prospect's (likely) pains as well as associated reasons, and knowledge of how your capabilities can address the likely pains. Awareness of your differentiators will also be important.

Note: Ideally, a database of standard Pain Sheets cataloged by common pains, job titles, capabilities, and/or industries would be most useful. Additionally, existing Pain Sheets should be updated periodically and new ones should be constructed to coincide with the introduction of any new offering or capability.

How to Build a Pain Sheet

There are seven primary steps involved in building a Pain Sheet:

Step 1 Determine the prospect to target (job title and industry).

Step 2 Anticipate the prospect's pain.

Step 3 Record reasons for the pain that your offerings or capabilities will address.

Step 4 Develop a series of "drill-down" or quantitative questions for each reason.

Step 5 Match your specific offerings or capabilities to the reasons they address.

Step 6 Create questions that enable buyers to visualize how your features or capabilities will help them.

Step 7 Develop questions that help explore the impact of pain on others.

 Step 1: Determine the prospect to target (job title and industry).
Step 2: Anticipate the prospect's pain.

These two steps can be accomplished more easily by reviewing a Key Player List, an initial Pain Chain, or information recorded in Account Profiles.

In your case, you should build your Pain Sheet by picking up where we left off with your opportunity. In Chapter 4, "How to Stimulate Interest with Prospects," you created business development job aids for a specific prospect (job title), targeting a potential pain. Assume that the prospect will admit to having the same pain—that will be the pain around which you should build your Pain Sheet.

 Step 3: Record reasons for the pain that your offerings or capabilities will address.

Brainstorm and record potential reasons for the pain that you believe your offering and capabilities will address. Keeping in mind that the Pain Sheet is a collection of diagnostic questions, phrase each reason in the form of a question (e.g., "Could one reason for your *[pain]* be because . . . ?").

Note: Reviewing your initial Pain Chain will help you to think through potential reasons for pain. See "Exercise: Build Your Pain Chain" in Chapter 3, "How to Conduct Effective Pre-call Planning and Research."

EXERCISE: BUILDING A PAIN SHEET, PART I

Activities

- Use the worksheet that follows. (*Note:* This worksheet gives only a portion of the actual Pain Sheet template, which will be shown in its entirety later in this chapter.)

- Record the prospect's job title, primary industry, and potential pain.

- Record reasons (attempt to identify four) for the potential pain that your offerings or capabilities will address.

Pain: _____
Job Title & Industry: _____
REASONS
Is it because . . . ; Today . . . ?
A.
B.
C.
D.

Step 4: Develop a series of "drill-down" or quantitative questions for each reason.

So, you've identified potential reasons for pain that you believe you can address? Great! But is each reason for pain something that the buyer wants to address? Does the reason contribute enough to the pain that the buyer can justify taking action? In other words, what is the scope of the pain or problem? Is it a $5,000 problem, a $50,000 problem, or a $500,000 problem? How do we know?

Quite simply, to determine the scope, we ask quantitative or drill-down questions for each of the reasons.

Nevertheless, *how* we ask is just as important as *what* we ask. The question, "How much does that *[reason for your pain]* cost you?" is certainly an easy question for you to ask, but it's not necessarily an easy question for a buyer to answer.

It reminds me of the old adage, "How do you eat an elephant? One bite at a time!" The same approach holds true when delving into "How much does that cost you?" It may be difficult for buyers to (excuse the pun) *digest* a big question like that; they find it more manageable to answer "bite-sized" questions.

Think of "bite-sized" questions much like simple algebra. There are variables you need to identify in order to determine an answer ($a \times b \times c = n$). Your job becomes getting answers to the variables so that you can determine n.

There are four benefits from asking these bite-sized questions:

1. The buyer can answer bite-sized questions more effortlessly.

2. The buyer can come to self-conclusion about the financial scope of the pain, because the buyer is the one providing the answers.

3. You get an opportunity to demonstrate your consultative side by leading the conversations with insightful questions.

4. You provide the buyer with logical reasons (value) to support what might be an emotional decision that he or she is making.

You should seek to provide logic to help your buyers justify a purchase that they are making based on emotion. Establishing quantifiable value through asking drill-down questions helps provide this logic.

The following example shows Steps 1 to 3 of How to Build a Pain Sheet completed.

Pain: Missing new account revenue targets **Job Title and Industry**: VP Sales, manufacturing
REASONS
Is it because . . . ; Today . . . ?
A. Salespeople spend too much time handling repeat business in existing accounts (i.e., they take orders instead of selling)?
B. Salespeople spend too much time answering frequently asked questions (FAQs) from current customers (instead of selling)?
C. Prospects are unaware of your promotions?
D. Salespeople fail to ask customers for referrals or leads?

Let's develop a series of drill-down questions for one of the reasons from this example. Let's use Reason B: "Salespeople spend too much time answering frequently asked questions (FAQs) from current customers."

Drill-down questions should help you systematically determine how much a reason contributes to the buyer's pain. They also should help to highlight the need for a capability that you have to offer and will eventually suggest. The following example illustrates a series of potential drill-down questions and how they might be answered.

Reason B:	Salespeople spend too much time answering frequently asked questions (FAQs) from current customers.	Buyer answers
■ What percentage of a salesperson's time is spent answering frequently asked questions?		15%
■ What amount of that time (15 percent) would you like them spending on answering FAQs?		0%
■ How many new customers did each salesperson bring in last year?		10
■ How many sales reps do you have?		50
■ What was the average annual revenue from each new customer?		$75,000
■ Would a salesperson be able to use that additional 15 percent of the time on other sales activities?		Yes
■ If reps had the additional time (15 percent), is it reasonable that each of them could bring in one new customer each year?		Yes

EXERCISE: BUILDING A PAIN SHEET, PART II

Activities

- Develop a series of drill-down questions for each of the reasons you recorded in the prior exercise.

- Use the Drill-Down Questions Worksheet that follows to record your work.

Note: When developing drill-down questions, make sure that all questions are phrased in such a manner that buyers' answers can easily be translated into annual figures. For example, "How often does that happen each year?" or "On average, how many times a month does that happen?" (then multiply the answer by 12).

Drill-Down Questions Worksheet

Reason A:
■
■
■
■

Reason B:
■
■
■
■

Reason C:
■
■
■
■

Reason D:
■
■
■
■

Step 5: Match specific features or capabilities of your offerings to the reasons they address.

At this point, you've identified reasons for potential pain that you believe your offering(s) will address. Now it is time to get more specific by determining exactly which of your offerings (features or capabilities) will help to alleviate the reason for pain.

EXERCISE: BUILDING A PAIN SHEET, PART III

Activities

- Identify the feature or capabilities of your offering(s) that address the buyer's reasons for pain.

- Record the name of each feature or capability in the worksheet that follows. Additionally, you may want to record the reasons again from "Exercise: Building a Pain Sheet, Part I" in the space provided.

REASONS		FEATURE OR CAPABILITY
A.	⇔	A.
B.	⇔	B.
C.	⇔	C.
D.	⇔	D.

You now know the buyer's pain, the reasons for the pain, and the features that the buyer needs. The buyer should be ready to buy, right? No! Not if the buyer doesn't understand and clearly visualize what the feature is going to allow him or her to do differently in the future. This is where you should attempt to articulate each feature in a manner that creates a vision for the buyer of how she or he will be able to perform a task differently after implementing the recommended offering.

 Step 6: Create questions that enable buyers to visualize how your features or capabilities will help them.

How do you create a capability vision? The simple answer is to create a word picture describing how the situation will be different utilizing your capabilities. In other words, you want to create a scenario in which buyers can see themselves or their world being better than it is today.

The following description indicates the approach for doing this.

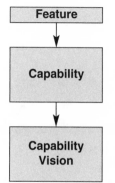

Feature — If possible, make sure the feature is a differentiator.

Capability — Elevate the *feature* to a *capability* by simply finishing the phrase:
"This feature allows you or someone in the organization to . . ."

Capability Vision — Elevate the *capability* into a *capability vision* by building upon *what* the capability allows to include a description of *who* in the buyer's organization will perform the function and *when* in time it will occur.

So, if we revisit our example from earlier, we'll see that the feature "Customer FAQ Page" addresses Reason B. It still needs to be articulated as a capability vision, though.

REASONS		FEATURE OR CAPABILITY
B. Salespeople spend too much time answering frequently asked questions (FAQs) from current customers.	⇔	**B.** Customer FAQ Page

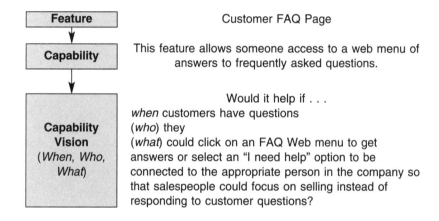

Feature	Customer FAQ Page
↓	
Capability	This feature allows someone access to a web menu of answers to frequently asked questions.
↓	
Capability Vision (*When, Who, What*)	Would it help if . . . *when* customers have questions (*who*) they (*what*) could click on an FAQ Web menu to get answers or select an "I need help" option to be connected to the appropriate person in the company so that salespeople could focus on selling instead of responding to customer questions?

When you successfully create capability visions, buyers can see how they will be able to do better in the future. In order to meet or exceed customer expectations, your offerings must consistently deliver the vision that has been established.

The cartoon that follows shows a salesperson guilty of overstating his offering's capabilities.

EXERCISE: BUILDING A PAIN SHEET, PART IV

Activities

- Use the Capability Vision Worksheet that follows.

- Recall each feature or capability identified in the prior exercise. Develop a vision that would address its corresponding reason for pain:
  - Elevate the feature to a capability by finishing the phrase: "This feature allows you to . . . *[do what]*."
  - Elevate the capability to a vision by building upon *what* the capability allows to include a description of *who* in the buyer's organization will perform the function and *when* in time it will occur.

Note: Capability visions need to be articulated in the form of a question for inclusion in the finalized Pain Sheet (e.g., "Would it help if . . . ?").

Capability Vision Worksheet

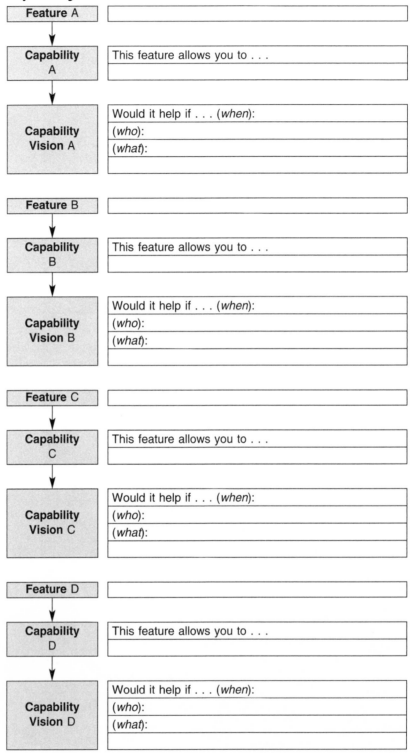

Feature A	

Capability A	This feature allows you to . . .

Capability Vision A	Would it help if . . . (*when*):
	(*who*):
	(*what*):

Feature B	

Capability B	This feature allows you to . . .

Capability Vision B	Would it help if . . . (*when*):
	(*who*):
	(*what*):

Feature C	

Capability C	This feature allows you to . . .

Capability Vision C	Would it help if . . . (*when*):
	(*who*):
	(*what*):

Feature D	

Capability D	This feature allows you to . . .

Capability Vision D	Would it help if . . . (*when*):
	(*who*):
	(*what*):

Step 7: Develop questions that help explore the impact of pain on others.

Impact questions explore the breadth and depth of a pain across the enterprise or a department. The reasons for asking these questions are to create a sense of urgency within the buyer and to identify other people whom you may need to make contact with. This is important in your quest to gain access to power. Salespeople that do not properly set expectations and create genuine visions fall into the trap of selling "vapor-ware," as demonstrated in the previous cartoon.

In our example, the Vice President of Sales's pain of "missing new account revenue targets" affects the Vice President of Finance's ability to meet both overall revenue targets and profitability goals. The series of questions for this situation may read:

- Is missing new account revenue targets causing missed overall revenue targets?

- Is that causing lower profits?

- Who is affected by this decline in profitability?

or

- Is the Vice President of Finance affected by this decline in profitability?

You want to explore the path of pain throughout the company or department. This can be accomplished by developing other impact questions.

EXERCISE: BUILDING A PAIN SHEET, PART V

Activities

- Develop a series of impact questions that will assist you in exploring the impact of pain upon other customer individuals.

- Use the Impact Questions Worksheet that follows to capture your work.

Notes:

- Record the impact in descending order, starting with the individual and pain directly caused by the pain of the targeted buyer.

- Refer to "Exercise: Build Your Pain Chain" in Chapter 3, "How to Conduct Effective Pre-call Planning and Research."

Impact Questions Worksheet

Is this _____ *[pain]* causing . . .
■   ?
■ ?
■ ?
■ ?
■ ?
Is the _____ *[job title]* impacted/concerned/affected?
■ ?
■ ?
■ ?
■ ?
■ ?
Is the _____ *[job title]* impacted/concerned/affected?
■ ?
■ ?
■ ?
■ ?
■ ?
Is the _____ *[job title]* impacted/concerned/affected?
■ ?
■ ?
■ ?
■ ?
■ ?
Is the _____ *[job title]* impacted/concerned/affected?

The Pain Sheet template is a summary document for capturing and compiling all of your work from the "Building a Pain Sheet" exercises into one job aid. This job aid could be used on a sales call or as part of your pre-call planning and research.

Pain Sheet Template

Pain: Job Title & Industry: Offering:		
REASONS	**IMPACT**	**CAPABILITIES**
Is it because . . . ; Today . . . ?	Is this [*pain*] causing . . . ?	What if . . . ; Would it help if . . . ?

A. [*Reason A*]
 	
(Include drill-down questions)
	• _____ ?
	• _____ ?
	• _____ ?
	
	Is the [*job title*] impacted?
		A. When:
		    Who:
		    What:

B. [*Reason B*]
 	
(Include drill-down questions)
	• _____ ?
	• _____ ?
	• _____ ?
	
	Is the [*job title*] impacted?
		B. When:
		    Who:
		    What:

C. [*Reason C*]
 	
(Include drill-down questions)
	• _____ ?
	• _____ ?
	• _____ ?
	
	Is the [*job title*] impacted?
		C. When:
		    Who:
		    What:

D. [*Reason D*]
 	
(Include drill-down questions)
		D. When:
		    Who:
		    What:

Remember that the Pain Sheet serves as a "situational fluency prompter" that enables you to ask control questions in the middle row of the 9 Block Vision Processing Model. An example of a completed Pain Sheet follows.

Pain Sheet Example

Pain: Missing new account revenue targets **Job Title & Industry:** VP Sales, manufacturing company **Offering:** e-Commerce Applications		
REASONS (R2)	**IMPACT (I2)**	**CAPABILITIES (C2)**
Is it because . . . ; Today . . . ?	Is this [*pain*] causing . . . ?	What if . . . ; Would it help if . . . ?
A. Salespeople spend too much time handling repeat business in existing accounts ("order taking" vs. selling)? • How much revenue is generated from this repeat business? • What percentage of that revenue requires no selling? • What percentage of a salesperson's time is spent on these activities? • How many salespeople have quotas [*#*]? • What is their average yearly quota [*$*]? • What percentage of their time could be used on selling new accounts? • Would the revenue increase by the same percentage?	• Missed overall revenue targets? $? #? %? • Lower profits? $? #? %? Is the Vice President of Finance concerned? • Impact on growth? $? #? %? • Declining stock price? $? #? %? Is the Chief Executive Officer affected?	A. *when*: wanting to place orders (*who*): your customers (*what*): could view inventory levels, place an order, and have it allocated and confirmed, all over the Internet?
B. Salespeople spend too much time answering FAQs from current customers? • What percentage of a salesperson's time is spent answering FAQs? • What amount of that time would you like your salespeople spending on answering FAQs? • What was the average # of new customers per sales rep last year? • What was the average $ per new customer? • What percentage of salespeople's time could be used on selling new accounts? • With that time, could reps bring in one new customer? • So, with _____ [#] reps that means _____ [$]?		B. *when*: customers have questions (*who*): they (*what*): could click on a FAQ Web menu to get answers or select an "I need help" option to be connected to the appropriate person in the company?
C. Prospects are unaware of your promotions? • What was the expected increase in revenue [$] from promotional campaigns last year? • What was actually achieved [$]? • What percentage of that shortfall would you attribute to prospects being unaware of promotions?		C. *when*: offering promotions (*who*): your salespeople (*what*): could create personalized messages and broadcast them to all of the prospects via e-mail?
D. Salespeople fail to ask customers for referrals or leads? • What percentage of customers are asked for referrals? • How many referrals [#] do you get per year? • What percentage of your revenue comes from these referrals? • If you asked all customers for referrals and leads, how many additional ones would you get?		D. *when*: visiting your Web site (*who*): your customers (*what*): could be prompted to submit referrals in exchange for discounts or promotional items?

Summary

Salespeople who help buyers admit pain, take the time to diagnose the pain, and help buyers visualize capabilities that will help them solve their pain have a high probability of winning the business. This approach works because

- It distinguishes those using it from traditional salespeople.
- Prospective buyers' expectations are properly set.
- The value of the solution is established in the mind of the buyers.

PART THREE

ENGAGING
IN ACTIVE
OPPORTUNITIES

CHAPTER 7

HOW TO SELL WHEN YOU ARE NOT FIRST

Why is it important to sell differently in opportunities where you are not there first from opportunities where you are?

Just because all men are created equal, does not mean that all sales opportunities are!

Think about it. If a buyer has a list of requirements, a time frame to make a decision, and a budget in place when you get invited to participate, what are the chances that the buyer doesn't already know who he or she wants to do business with?

When you are not first, not only does the buyer usually want you to respond to the list of requirements in a structured fashion, but the buyer also keeps you an arm's length away and makes you play by rules that were most likely established by your competitor. No, thank you—I think I'll decide for myself which competitive strategy and tactics will give me the best chance of winning against an established list of biased requirements, or if I should even compete at all.

In this chapter, you'll find principles, exercises, and job aids for qualifying opportunities and determining the best competitive strategy and approach. Solution Selling job aids that will help you accomplish these tasks are

**Opportunity Assessment
Worksheet**

**Competitive Strategy
Selector**

Traditional qualification is just that—too traditional, and in today's world not very effective. What you are about to read and experience is a much more current and accurate approach to this critical component of selling.

The following exercise is one that I have used in many of my Solution Selling workshops. Its purpose is to show how traditional qualification approaches may be misleading.

EXERCISE: QUALIFICATION

- Read each of the five scenarios that follow. In each scenario, the statements are intended to represent quotes from prospective buyers.

- Record what you believe are your chances of winning based on the bulleted information provided for each opportunity (0 to 100 percent).

Scenario	Win %
1. ■ I have shared my pain with you. ■ Your offering is exactly what I'm looking for, and it adds value. ■ You helped me to establish the requirements of my project. ■ Your overall price is 5 percent lower than your average competitor's. ■ Your company's reputation for implementation support is remarkable.	_____ %
2. ■ I have shared my pain with you. ■ Your offering is viewed as a commodity but is still very valuable to me. ■ I have budgeted for this project. ■ You are not the first vendor I've talked to, but if you can come down on your price by 10 percent, you'll win the business.	_____ %
3. ■ I'll make the decision soon because my time frame dictates that I select the vendor of choice by the end of this month. ■ You obviously have the best offering, but your price is more than I had budgeted for. ■ I don't necessarily have to select the lowest bid, but I do need to be able to tell the senior management team that I came away with some type of price concession while getting into our budget parameters.	_____ %
4. ■ Your product and services match my needs very well. ■ I have budgeted for this project; however, the budget—which is cast in stone—is 10 percent less than your quoted price to me, so I need you to help me out here. ■ I am the committee chairperson heading the decision. ■ I have no choice but to make a decision on this by quarter's end.	_____ %
5. ■ The company that usually provides me with these services has not been invited to bid; I want new thinking, and your organization fits that bill. ■ You've proved that you truly understand my business and my admitted pain. ■ I really mean it when I say that this business is yours if you can reduce the overall project cost by 15 percent.	_____ %

Now, total the win percentage for all five scenarios. Is it above 100 percent? Is it above 150 percent? Is it above 200 percent? What about over 250 percent?

What if I told you that all five scenarios involved competing vendors for one project?

What's the point that I'm making here? Savvy buyers will tell you what you want to hear in order to get the best deal. In some instances, their purpose may be to get price concessions from "column fodder" vendors in order to then get a lower quote from the desired vendor. In other instances, buyers may tell the salesperson what he or she wants to hear in order to learn more about the offerings and services, even though they have no intention of buying.

Some time ago, I was speaking with a prospect. He described in length how his sales team was faced with an inability to qualify opportunities. I challenged him with the idea that his team didn't have a problem with qualifying opportunities, but rather a problem with *disqualifying* opportunities.

The skill of *qualification* is the ability to help bring an opportunity to an established standard. *Disqualification* is the ability to disengage from an opportunity if it does not meet the standard.

The Biggest Myth of Qualification

All over the world, I have taught Solution Selling workshops, attended consulting engagements, and spoken at corporate sales meetings for clients whose sales organizations were as different as their international cultures. Ironically, there is one question that I ask various groups that invariably gets the same universal answer. The question is, "What elements make an opportunity qualified?" Without too much variance, the answers I hear most often are

- *Budget* The project is funded.

- *Authority* A decision maker is in place within the prospective buyer's organization.

- *Need/fit* Your offerings match the list of requirements.

- *Time frame* The prospective buyer has identified a date by which the purchase decision must be made.

Some people refer to these four elements simply as BANT. I would contend that using BANT as your sole qualification method may cause you to stay in opportunities that are better qualified for someone else.

Don't get me wrong—the elements of BANT are very important in any selling engagement. However, a buyer who can give you answers to these four elements can probably tell you the answer to the more important fifth question—*whom he or she has decided to buy from.* They must be "down the road a bit" in their buying process, and you are being brought into the situation late—you're column fodder.

Important information concerning BANT is critical for a salesperson to discover *during a sell cycle,* but real opportunity qualification should include some additional criteria as well.

Additional Qualification Criteria— The Successful Sales Formula

The following formula expands the basis for qualifying opportunities. In addition to BANT, if you don't have an affirmative answer to each variable, then the chance of a successful sale is zero.

Pain × Power × Vision × Value × Control = $uccessful $ale

In Chapter 3 we discussed the concept of buyer pain. The basic principle "no pain, no change" speaks volumes about why this element is so critical to the successful sales formula. High-priority pain, which also includes potential missed opportunities, helps answer the question, "Is the customer likely to take action?"

Although we'll discuss the concept of power sponsors in more depth in Chapter 10, the term *power* can be defined quite simply as the person within the buying organization with the ability to make or influence the purchasing decision.

We touched on *vision* and *value* in the prior chapter. (Vision means that the prospective buyer must understand what your offering will allow her or him to do, but must also be able to visualize doing something different in the future. Value means that the prospective buyer must grasp the quantifiable value that he or she will be receiving by making an investment in your offering.)

The term *control* might sound a bit manipulative, but it is really about attempting to exert control within the buying process, not over the buyer. We'll look at this in detail in Chapter 10.

Opportunity Assessment

Qualification does not happen just once—it is a continuous process. Opportunities should be periodically reassessed and qualified to ensure that they meet your qualification criteria. You may find that a once-qualified opportunity has become unqualified as a result of changes within the buying organization or other factors outside of your control. Remember, the only thing wrong about being wrong is staying wrong!

Within Solution Selling we have created a job aid that we call the Opportunity Assessment Worksheet. Many people need a third party or an objective resource to assist them with qualification.

 Opportunity Assessment Worksheet

Overview
The Opportunity Assessment Worksheet is a qualification model consisting of 25 questions in five categories (pain, power, vision, value, and control). This scalable set of opportunity-focused questions helps you to objectively make an early (and continuing) qualification decision about whether to pursue an opportunity.

Where/How Used

The Opportunity Assessment Worksheet should be used to answer critical questions at strategic points in the life of an opportunity, including "Should we compete?" and "Can we win?"

What You Should Achieve

The user should answer the assessment honestly and objectively to determine

- What information is known

- What information is not known

- The scope of the activity and resources required to improve the status of the opportunity so that an engagement or disengagement decision can be made

Input Required

Information gained from conversations, research, and all known available data that might affect the current situation.

Opportunity Assessment Worksheet

	Opportunity Assessment Worksheet		Assessment date: _____		
	Answer key: (Y) Yes, (N) No, or (?) Unsure			Us	Comp
	★ = "Quick Five" assessment questions				
★	*Pain* "Is the customer likely to act?"	★			
1	Has high-priority pain or potential pain been identified?				
2	Have *we* validated the pain with the owner(s)?				
3	Do *we* understand how others are impacted by the pain?				
4	Is there a budget in place?				
5	Is there a time frame to address the pain?				
★	*Power* "Are *we* aligned with the right people to win?"	★			
6	Do *we* understand the roles of the key players for this opportunity?				
7	Do *we* understand who will influence the decision and how?				
8	Are *we* connected to the people in power?				
9	Do *we* have the support of the key players?				
10	Are *we* connected to the people with access to funds?				
★	*Vision* "Does the customer prefer *our* offering?"	★			
11	Did *we* help establish the initial requirements?				
12	Does *our* offering fit the customer's needs/requirements?				
13	Have *we* created or reengineered a differentiated vision for the key players?				
14	Do the key players support *our* solution approach?				
★	*Value* "Does *our* offering provide mutual value?"	★			
15	Do *we* understand the benefit to each key player and the corporation?				
16	Have the key players quantified and articulated the benefits of *our* offering to *us*?				
17	Has a (corporate) value analysis been agreed upon?				
18	Does the value analysis warrant access to funds?				
19	Is there sufficient value to *us*? Is the opportunity profitable? Is it strategic?				
★	*Control* "Can *we* control the buying process?"	★			
20	Do *we* understand the decision-making process and the criteria for the key players?				
21	Do *we* understand the proof and satisfaction requirements for the key players?				
22	Do *we* understand the customer's buying practices, policies, and procedures?				
23	Has the customer agreed to an evaluation process with *us*?				
24	Can *we* control the evaluation process?				
25	Can *we* successfully manage *our* risk?				

Some things to recognize about the Opportunity Assessment Worksheet:

- The ratings (yes, no, and unsure) allow the salesperson to determine his or her own status for each question as well as allow for a comparison against competition. (*Note:* Additional columns for competitive analysis could certainly be added.)

- The "Quick Five" assessment questions (found in the darkened rows of the Opportunity Assessment Worksheet) also provide a location for the salesperson to rate her or his status and also that of possible competitors.

- The space provided for "assessment date" helps salespeople and managers determine the age of the information gathered. It becomes especially useful when a salesperson performs later assessments to determine progress or lack thereof.

- The Opportunity Assessment Worksheet should not be viewed as a scorecard (i.e., more "yes" ratings for one vendor does not equate to a win). It helps the salesperson objectively determine what she or he knows, doesn't know, and needs to know.

- It is reasonable to expect answers of "unsure" to several questions early in the sell cycle, when there is more information to be uncovered.

- Most of the 25 questions have been written in such a manner that all references to your organization (the word *our* or *we*) are in italics. During any competitive assessment, those words should be replaced by *they* or *their* to answer each question from the perspective of the competition.

 For someone selling in a transaction-based environment where opportunities are turned over quickly or someone who has a full pipeline of many opportunities, it may make sense to use the successful sale formula as a quick opportunity assessment ("The Quick Five")

 Pain "Is the customer likely to act?"

Power "Are *you* aligned with the right people to win?"

Vision "Does the customer prefer *your* offering?"

Value "Does *your* offering provide mutual value?"

Control "Can *you* control the buying process?"

Those five questions may be sufficient for qualifying opportunities in some selling environments, but for more complex opportunities, a deeper level of questions may need to be answered. The 25 questions provide that deeper level of assessment within the framework of the successful sale formula.

EXERCISE: ASSESS YOUR OPPORTUNITY
Activities

- Use the Opportunity Assessment Worksheet shown previously.

- If your opportunity originated as an active one, identify your competition and complete the worksheet, considering all information you have available.

- If your opportunity originated from uncovering latent pain, identify your potential competition and complete the worksheet, making assumptions where necessary.

Competitive Strategies

The results of your opportunity assessment will guide you to the most appropriate competitive strategy—the one that will give you the best chance to win the business. Competitive strategies help you to determine what kinds of actions you will take to secure the business. They enable you to select the right tactics and apply the right resources.

There are five competitive strategies:

- Preemptive
- Head-to-head
- End around
- Divide and conquer
- Stall

Preemptive Strategy

If you helped the prospect uncover a latent pain, then you have preempted your competition in a new opportunity. The preemptive competitive strategy is the most powerful one—you have the greatest chance to win business when you have no competition!

The focus of your assessment at this point should be less on competition and more on determining whether the opportunity is worth pursuing. The following chart provides some insight into what you should consider when making a preemptive engagement decision.

Preemptive	
Description: This strategy, although not a competitive strategy in the purest sense, is the most desired strategy when you consider the advantages of initiating an opportunity instead of reacting to one. The largest hurdle for salespeople and sales managers to overcome is that this approach requires prospecting instead of aggressively waiting by the phone.	
Use this strategy when you can answer yes to the following key questions:	
■ Did you identify latent pain? ■ Has high-priority pain been admitted to you by a customer key player? ■ Can you establish business impact on others and create visions of how their issues may be addressed?	
Tactics	**Pros and Cons**
■ Develop needs and decision criteria ■ Create a natural bond through joint discovery ■ Establish the impact upon other customer key players ■ Create unique, differentiated visions of your solution ■ Articulate the value of your offering	**Pro:** Your win odds increase dramatically when you help establish the requirements **Con:** The sell cycle can be longer

If you engage in an opportunity after the buyer has established a vision of a solution (an active opportunity), then you'll need to select one of four competitive strategies. On the next few pages, you'll see some useful criteria for choosing the best competitive strategy when you're not first.

Head-to-Head Strategy

This is the default strategy used by most salespeople, and the most obvious. It is also the easiest competitive strategy to defeat, if one doesn't have overwhelming advantages.

Head-to-Head	
Description: In this strategy, two organizations compete in a "head-to-head" or direct fashion—one might say feature-to-feature. Buyers like us to compete this way. It allows them to conduct a comparison analysis—comparing apples to apples. It is the strategy most often used by salespeople; it is also the strategy that salespeople lose with the most often. Sun-Tzu, the famous Chinese philosopher and military general, said that at least a 3:1 advantage is required when competing in a head-to-head fashion.	

Use this strategy when you can answer yes to the following key questions:
■ Has the customer established its requirements and/or decision criteria? Is there a budget? Is there a time frame?
■ Can your offering address all or most of the requirements and/or decision criteria?
■ Do you have an established, apparent (3:1) advantage from the customer's perspective?

Tactics	Pros and Cons

■ Prioritize requirements and/or criteria
■ Capitalize on superiority of your
  ■ Offering
  ■ Reputation
  ■ Established base
	Pro: Possible short sell cycle, but only if you have an obvious 3-to-1 advantage in price, performance, or company reputation that is acknowledged by the buyer
	Con: May be won at a high cost of sale

End Around Strategy

If you cannot answer yes to all of the key questions for a head-to-head strategy, you might want to consider the end around strategy. In today's business environment, it's rare for a sales organization to have a 3:1 advantage from the buyer's perspective. Often I will recommend the end around strategy as a starting point so that salespeople don't mislead themselves into thinking that they have a 3:1 advantage and begin with the wrong competitive strategy.

End Around	
Description: In this strategy, one organization attempts to change the rules of the game in order to compete more effectively. This strategy is also referred to as vision reengineering. The classic execution of this strategy is where the Column B vendor attempts to introduce a valuable differentiating feature into a list of defined requirements, knowing that the preferred vendor, Column A, does not have the same feature or offering established as part of the requirements list.	

Use this strategy when you can answer yes to the following key question:
■ Can you create differentiated value and change or grow the requirements or decision criteria?

Tactics	Pros and Cons

■ Understand the current requirements and decision criteria
■ Neutralize the competition
■ Reengineer the customer's original vision:
  ■ By adding features or offering(s) to the list of requirements that are differentiators
  ■ By establishing the unique, quantifiable value of the newly introduced features or offering(s)
  ■ By minimizing the need for a competing requirement if true value for it does not exist
	Pro: The buying decision can sometimes be made rapidly
	Con: You may have difficulty gaining access to power

Divide and Conquer Strategy

If you cannot answer yes to the key question for the end around strategy, you might want to consider the divide and conquer strategy.

Divide and Conquer	
Description: This strategy is used when you cannot meet all of the defined requirements, but you can perform one of the functions in an exceptional manner. Pursue only the part of the business that can be won. For example, if your organization is a total solution provider, you may bid on an entire project, only to realize that the price and functionality of parts of your solution aren't competitive. You may still bid on a portion of the opportunity, knowing that it is a strength of yours. Some people refer to this as "finding a niche."	

Use this strategy when you can answer yes to the following key question:
■ Can you address *part* of the requirements or decision criteria?

Tactics	Pros and Cons
■ Understand the current requirements and decision criteria ■ Identify solution components that you can address ■ Highlight the quantifiable value and advantage of the addressable component	**Pro**: Possible base for future growth **Con**: Reduced total revenue potential and presence in the opportunity or account

Stall Strategy

If you cannot answer yes to the key question for the divide and conquer strategy, you might want to consider the stall strategy as a last resort.

Stall	
Description: This fallback position encourages the buyer to delay making a purchasing decision until the company executing the stall approach can present its offering. Most companies that can successfully use this approach must have a great deal of market share or brand recognition. *Note:* Some companies may make prerelease announcements to stave off their competitors. Be sure to have firsthand knowledge of any legal issues relevant today concerning making prerelease statements and illegal business practices.	

Use this strategy when you can answer yes to the following key question:
■ Will you be able to address the requirements and decision criteria and/or form relationships with power in the future?

Tactics	**Pros and Cons**
■ Understand the current requirements and decision criteria ■ Assess the potential to win later ■ Assess your exposure if the opportunity is delayed ■ Highlight potential quantifiable value to the customer from waiting ■ Establish additional support of customer key players while in a state of stall	**Pro:** Keeps the opportunity alive and denies it to competitors **Con:** May be perceived as not focused on customer issues

To help you make a sound competitive strategy decision, all of these considerations have been compiled into a map. This job aid is known as the Competitive Strategy Selector.

 Competitive Strategy Selector

Overview
The Competitive Strategy Selector provides key questions that should be answered to direct the salesperson (and the account

team) in selecting the competitive strategy to attempt to employ for the given opportunity, and also offers suggested supporting tactics.

Where/How Used

Depending on the opportunity's origin (i.e., a latent pain opportunity or an active opportunity), the strategy selected will vary. If the opportunity is latent, by default the team has engaged in a preemptive strategy. If the opportunity is of the active variety, the team should consider some key questions to determine exactly which competitive strategy (head-to-head, end around, divide and conquer, or stall) to use.

What You Should Achieve

You should be able to make a strategy decision. If the choice is to engage, then you should determine the strategy to use, determine specific tactics for executing the strategy, and weigh the pros and cons associated with the selected strategy and tactics. The chosen strategy should be communicated to the entire sales team.

Input Required

Enough knowledge of the account or opportunity origin to answer the initial key questions.

Competitive Strategy Selector

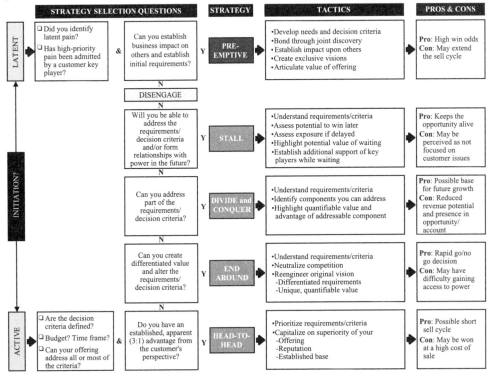

Now you should give it a try. Assess your opportunity and determine the most effective strategy with which to compete. The exercises that follow will help you accomplish this.

EXERCISE: SELECT YOUR COMPETITIVE STRATEGY

Activities

- Determine which competitive strategy you should engage in (or the preemptive strategy, if applicable), using the answers from the Opportunity Assessment Worksheet.

- Determine and record exposures that exist from the assessment.

- Determine and record the tactics from the Competitive Strategy Selector that will help address each exposure if properly executed.

- Determine and record additional tactics that will be needed to address your exposures.

- Use the Action Plan Worksheet that follows to capture your work.

Action Plan Worksheet

Exposure:
Tactic →
Tactic →
Tactic →
Tactic →
Exposure:
Tactic →
Tactic →
Tactic →
Tactic →
Exposure:
Tactic →
Tactic →
Tactic →
Tactic →
Exposure:
Tactic →
Tactic →
Tactic →
Tactic →

Summary

Not all sales opportunities are created equal. The strategy and supporting tactics that you use will differ—assuming that you decide to engage in an opportunity at all. If your assessment indicates that you have little chance of winning, then the best decision is not to compete.

You've already been exposed to the 9 Block Vision Processing Model for creating visions. In the next chapter, we are going to look at navigating the same model, but in a different sequence (vision reengineering), to carry out the end around competitive strategy. The 9 Block Vision Processing Model for Vision Reengineering also serves as a useful framework for having customer conversations that help you execute the tactics of the divide and conquer and stall strategies.

CHAPTER 8

HOW TO REENGINEER A VISION OF A SOLUTION

Why is reengineering a vision of a solution important?

In Chapter 2, I indicated that salespeople encounter active opportunities the majority of the time, instead of initiating them. They respond to a preestablished list of requirements defined by the buyer and the preferred provider—Company A. That leaves low win odds for all organizations responding to the list of established requirements. All things being equal, the organizations that were invited in late have to overcome a bond of joint discovery formed between the buyer and Company A.

How do you overcome this bond? As the tactics in the Competitive Strategy Selector suggest, you must introduce differentiators that are unique and provide quantifiable value. Additionally, the need to change or expand the list of established requirements has to be the buyer's idea.

In this chapter, you'll find principles, exercises, and job aids that help you to persuade buyers that they need your valued differentiators, thereby reengineering the buyers' existing vision of a solution. Those Solution Selling job aids are

9 Block Vision Processing Model for Vision Reengineering	Pain Sheet	RFP Initial Response Letter	RFP Executive Summary

The ability to reengineer a buyer's existing vision of a solution is an important skill and quite different from creating an original vision of a solution with a buyer. This is a challenge for a lot of salespeople. Too often, they engage in the same selling tactics regardless of the opportunity's origin.

There are multiple ways you might get involved in an active opportunity:

- By pursuing a latent pain opportunity, only to find out that the buyer already has a vision

- By unexpectedly receiving a request for a proposal (RFP) asking you to bid on an established list of requirements

- By receiving a request for information (RFI) from a buyer who is looking to develop an idea of what he or she needs before sending it out to bid

In any scenario where you are late into the opportunity, you have to earn the right to reengineer the buying vision. To earn this right, you must follow this basic principle: *make yourself equal before you make yourself different.*

> **BASIC PRINCIPLE**
>
> MAKE YOURSELF EQUAL BEFORE YOU MAKE YOURSELF DIFFERENT

People are generally fond of their own ideas. There is a sense of ownership attached to the development of an idea. Consequently, most people don't like to be told that their ideas are bad ones.

Sometimes a prospective buyer shares an idea with us (maybe a vision influenced by a competitor), and we rush to explain why the buyer is wrong or why this is a poor decision. Instead, <u>build empathy with your buyer</u>. *First* seek to understand the buyer's existing vision *before* you attempt to add to it or change it. Psychologically, the buyer will be more willing to engage in dialogue that focuses on topics outside of the original vision once the buyer feels that you understand his or her current perspective.

"Making yourself equal before you make yourself different" is a prerequisite to reengineering existing visions. Keep this principle in mind as we look at the vision reengineering structure of the 9 Block Vision Processing Model.

If you are already familiar with the 9 Block Vision Processing Model for Vision Reengineering and would like to skip ahead to the application portion, go to the section in this chapter entitled "Differentiation."

However, if you skipped to this section (Part Three, "Engaging in Active Opportunities") because you deal primarily with active opportunities, I would encourage you to read Chapter 6, "How to Diagnose and Create a Vision of a Solution." It provides an important baseline of information on the 9 Block Vision Processing Model that I will build upon in the rest of this chapter.

9 Block Vision Processing Model—Vision Reengineering

Overview

The 9 Block Vision Processing Model for Vision Reengineering is a buyer-focused questioning model. It is used to introduce differentiating capabilities while leading a buyer to self-conclusion of a reengineered vision of a solution.

Where/How Used

The framework of the 9 Block Vision Processing Model is derived by employing three types of questions:

- Open questions

- Control questions

- Confirming questions

These questions are used to cover three significant areas of exploration:

- Diagnosis of reasons for pain

- Exploration of the impact of pain on others

- Help in visualizing the capabilities needed

For active opportunities, a vision must be reengineered. You will need to navigate the model in a different sequence from that used in vision creation.

What You Should Achieve

Successful use of the 9 Block Vision Processing Model for Vision Reengineering should result in the prospective buyer expanding or changing her or his original vision. If the new list of requirements includes your differentiated capabilities, then you have successfully reengineered the vision.

Input Required

Pain Sheets are situationally specific job aids that help prompt a salesperson to ask intelligent, control-oriented questions in the control row of the 9 Block Vision Processing Model. Pain Sheets used in vision reengineering should stress key differentiators.

9 Block Vision Processing Model—Vision Reengineering

	DIAGNOSE REASONS	EXPLORE IMPACT	VISUALIZE CAPABILITIES
PAIN ───────────── CURRENT VISION			
OPEN	R1 (3) "How do you do 'it' today without this capability?"	I1 (6) "Besides yourself, WHO in your organization is impacted by this (pain) and HOW are they impacted?"	C1 (1) "How do you see yourself using this (repeat buyer initial vision)...?"
CONTROL	R2 (4) "Today...?"	I2 (7) "Is this (pain) causing...?" "If so, would (title) also be concerned?"	C2 (2) "Are you also looking for a way to...?" "Would it help if you also had a way to...?"
CONFIRM	R3 (5) "So, the way you do it today is... Is that correct?"	I3 (8) "From what I just heard... (repeat the WHO and HOW), it sounds like this is not just your problem, but a _____ problem! Is that correct?"	C3 (9) "...When you called you were looking at (original "vision"). Today, you also said you needed... (capability visions). If you had...could you (verbalize goal)?"
		BUYING VISION	

The Pain Sheet introduced in Chapter 6 for vision creation can also be used in vision reengineering; however, the components of the Pain Sheet will be used in a different sequence, just as the vision processing model's sequence has changed.

Differentiation

To succeed in vision reengineering, you must introduce those capabilities that you have that are truly unique or different from your competition. One way to identify differentiators is to plot your unique features and capabilities on a differentiation grid, as demonstrated in the following example. The features and capabilities that fall in the upper right quadrant are the ones you should use to try to reengineer the buyer's vision.

The features that demonstrate the greatest differentiation and resolve reasons for potential pain should be developed into capability vision questions and placed on the Pain Sheet in order of importance—the best differentiating capabilities first.

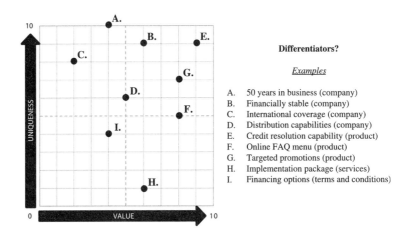

Differentiators?

Examples

A. 50 years in business (company)
B. Financially stable (company)
C. International coverage (company)
D. Distribution capabilities (company)
E. Credit resolution capability (product)
F. Online FAQ menu (product)
G. Targeted promotions (product)
H. Implementation package (services)
I. Financing options (terms and conditions)

Also, don't think of differentiators as being limited to features of a product or service. You probably have company differentiators (e.g., tenure, financial stability, breadth of solutions), and the experience (e.g., industry expertise) you bring to a particular situation may also be a differentiator. Sometimes your contractual terms and conditions may be a differentiator (e.g., financing options). Consider these as you perform this next exercise.

EXERCISE: DETERMINE YOUR DIFFERENTIATORS

Activities

- Develop a list of your most valued differentiating features or capabilities.

- Rate each of them in terms of uniqueness and value to see where they stand in general comparison to competitive or industry norms or in comparison to a specific competitor (0 = no value, no uniqueness; 5 = average in comparison to the industry norm; 10 = highest value, most uniqueness).

- Use the following worksheets to capture your work.

Features or Capabilities
A.
B.
C.
D.
E.
F.
G.
H.
I.
J.

Differentiation Grid

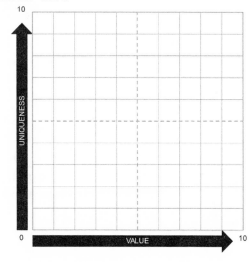

Note: You may want to revisit "Exercise: Building a Pain Sheet, Part IV" (Chapter 6) and see how many of the capability visions developed include the key differentiators.

Requests for Proposal (RFP)

As I mentioned at the beginning of this chapter, some of the ways you might get involved in active opportunities are to receive a request for proposal (RFP), a request for information (RFI), or a tender request asking for information or a bid on an established list of requirements.

The basic principle that I would like you to accept is this: If you did not help write the RFP's requirements, the odds of your winning these opportunities are low. With this in mind, you will need to select the correct competitive strategy and follow it up with tactics that will improve your chances of winning. In most instances, the best strategy for RFP's is the end around, and the best tactic will be vision reengineering.

So why do salespeople respond to RFPs when the odds of winning are so low? I believe there are three main reasons for this, as shown here. Review them and honestly ask yourself if you are guilty of ever falling into any of these three categories.

"Pick low-hanging fruit" Although this phrase is a cliché, it has a lot of merit as it relates to salespeople pursuing potential opportunities. Often salespeople will focus their time and energy on opportunities that fall into their lap and appear to require little effort.

 *The dreaded alternative is prospecting* It is a fact of human nature that most of us do not like rejection. Prospecting is a numbers game that results in many rejections by prospects. Salespeople may avoid real prospecting activities until the pipeline dries up and all they are left with is responding to active RFPs.

"Blind qualification" We've discussed the elements of a qualified opportunity. Blind qualification happens when salespeople talk themselves into believing that an opportunity is qualified while ignoring important qualification questions.

If any of these sound familiar, then you might want to consider the real cost of responding to RFPs. As a matter of fact, one of the first things I ask clients to do when they describe themselves as "proposal response factories" is to objectively consider the cost and success rate of their responses to RFPs.

Responding to RFPs—Is It Worth It?

As with anything, there will always be an exception to the rule. I have had clients who have been remarkably successful at responding to unsolicited RFPs, but in most of those cases the client had overwhelming market share and a vastly superior offering. For most other organizations that habitually respond to RFPs and get poor results—stop the madness. Consider these important questions when deciding if your organization should make a practice of responding to RFPs:

- How many proposals do you and/or your team respond to in a year? _____

- What is the average number of people that it takes to work on one proposal? _____

- What is the average number of hours that each person works on one proposal? _____

- What is the average operational cost of a "person-hour"? $_____

- What is the lost opportunity cost? $_____

These questions will tell you the average cost to your organization of responding to one RFP, but let's also consider the following:

- What is your win rate on responding to proposals? _____%

- What is the average revenue attainment from a win? $_____

- What is the profit margin on that revenue attainment? _____%

Is it worth it? I generally think it is not. The win rate and the high opportunity cost tell me that this isn't the most productive use of resources. However, if you are going to respond to RFPs, something has to change in order for you to win. I recommend deploying the end around competitive strategy and following these eight specific tactical steps:

Tactical Step 1 Call the sender and offer to respond to the RFP in exchange for interviews with key players impacted by the scope of the project. (If this is granted, go to Tactical Step 4.)

Tactical Step 2 If your request for a meeting is denied, send an e-mail or letter to the sender stating that it will be impossible for you to respond to the RFP without the interviews (see the RFP Initial Response Letter).

Tactical Step 3 When the sender calls you again, repeat the offer to respond to the RFP in exchange for the interviews. If this is declined, tactfully withdraw from the opportunity.

Tactical Step 4 If you are granted an interview, ask each key player impacted by the scope of the project this question: What are the two primary issues behind the project? (You're trying to get the person to admit pains so that you can begin to reengineer the buying visions with your unique differentiators.)

Tactical Step 5 Assuming that interviews were granted, prepare your response to the RFP as agreed.

Tactical Step 6 Write a cover letter to the person controlling the RFP and send it with the proposal. Specifically point to the executive summary (see RFP Executive Summary) and how it documents the buying vision of each line executive that you spoke with.

Tactical Step 7 Based upon your interviews, write an executive summary that specifically points out how your proposed solution addresses the unique capabilities needed to solve the critical business issues identified by each key player.

Tactical Step 8 Send copies of the cover letter and your RFP response to the key players with whom you had the best rapport.

 ## RFP Initial Response Letter

Overview
The RFP Initial Response Letter is a letter or e-mail sent by you that attempts to suggest a bargain in which you will respond to the RFP in exchange for first meeting with the key players impacted by the scope of the project.

Where/How Used
The RFP Initial Response Letter is used only after the RFP sender has denied a verbal request by you to meet with the customer key players impacted by the scope of the project.

The RFP Initial Response Letter is used to document your request and to make a calculated statement to the buyer that suggests that your organization has a practice of responding to RFPs only after you've met with the key players impacted by the project, and that this practice is in the best interest of the buyer's organization.

What You Should Achieve
The RFP Initial Response Letter should achieve one of two results:

1. You are granted access to the desired key players in order to conduct vision processing interviews.

2. The RFP sender responds with a final denial, at which point you have to decide whether to respond to the RFP or to disengage.

Input Required

The important input will be deciding which of the key players will need to be interviewed.

Note: This approach should be supported by senior executives within your organization because it challenges traditional approaches to handling RFPs.

See the template for the RFP Initial Response Letter in Appendix B, "Solution Selling Job Aid Templates."

 RFP Executive Summary

Overview

The RFP Executive Summary highlights additional capabilities needed by the buying organization that are not found in the scope of its current RFP.

Where/How Used

The RFP Executive Summary is sent to the RFP sender and the key players met with during the interviews (negotiated via the RFP Initial Response Letter). The RFP Executive Summary should be placed at the beginning of the RFP response or used as a cover letter that accompanies the final proposal.

The RFP Executive Summary summarizes additional capabilities needed by the key players that were uncovered during the vision processing conversations that took place during the agreed-upon interviews.

What You Should Achieve
The intent of the RFP Executive Summary is to stress the importance of the additional capabilities needed from the perspective of the key players. The desire is to catch the attention of the RFP sender and/or consultant(s) in order to have the initial requirements of the RFP expanded or changed to include these additional capabilities.

Input Required
The critical input into the RFP Executive Summary is the highlighting of your differentiating capabilities needed by the key players.

See the template for the RFP Executive Summary in Appendix B, "Solution Selling Job Aid Templates."

Summary

When you engage in active opportunities or respond to requests for proposal, the task is difficult and the odds of winning are low. Opportunity assessments are key to making good decisions. You have to honestly assess your chances of winning and engage only in those opportunities that are most qualified. Success hinges on your ability to diagnose pain and reengineer the buyer's visions around your unique capabilities.

PART FOUR

QUALIFYING, CONTROLLING, AND CLOSING OPPORTUNITIES

CHAPTER 9

HOW TO GAIN ACCESS TO POWER

Why is gaining access to power important?

The fundamental reason why gaining access to power is so important is that people with power ultimately influence or directly affect every decision that is made. For this reason alone, you should strive to gain access to power in every selling situation.

Have you ever tried to share a really funny story with someone who didn't see the humor in it? In that situation, did you find that person looking at you with a blank stare as if to say, "This is what you wanted to share with me?" To which you reply, "Well, you had to be there."

Often that is exactly what happens when a salesperson leaves the job of "selling" to power—the ultimate decision makers—in the hands of an internal sponsor. What is the best thing you hope will happen when you turn over this responsibility to the internal sponsor? You hope that the sponsor will articulate the problem, the vision, and the value just as you would. However, this rarely happens, because sponsors typically don't have the situational knowledge or the experience of previously solving the problems with the unique capabilities that you can provide.

Ultimately, gaining access to power helps shorten sell cycles and improves your chances of winning. Remember the formula: Pain × Power × Vision × Value × Control = Successful Sale. Gaining access to power is a key qualifier in every sales situation.

In this chapter, you'll find principles, exercises, and job aids that help you gain access to power. Those Solution Selling job aids are

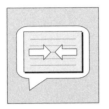
Strategic Alignment Prompter (Steps 5–7a)

Sponsor Letter (Vision Creation)

Sponsor Letter (Reengineering)

The use of these job aids will assist you in gaining access to a power sponsor. The alternative is to attempt to *sell* at a level with someone who can't buy—our next basic principle.

BASIC PRINCIPLE

YOU CAN'T SELL TO SOMEONE WHO CAN'T BUY

You can spend a lot of time, money, and resources with prospective buyers who show interest and are willing to gather coworkers for meetings and demonstrations—*but* who can't make a commitment or a purchasing decision. You must

- Minimize the amount of time you spend with people who lack the influence or the authority to make buying decisions by qualifying prospective buyers early in the sales process.

- Bargain for access to power when necessary by leveraging your assets and resources—quid pro quo.

- Disengage from the person or opportunity when access to power is denied. Move from the sponsor to the power sponsor as quickly as possible.

In Chapter 5, I introduced the Strategic Alignment Prompter as a seven-step guide that helps you align your selling activities with the buying process. We've looked specifically at the first four steps of the Strategic Alignment Prompter:

Step 1 Establish rapport

Step 2 Introduce the call

Step 3 Get pain admitted

Step 4 Develop customer needs (vision creation or vision reengineering)

In this chapter, well pick up with the steps of the Strategic Alignment Prompter that help you gain access to power. Those steps are

Step 5 Gain agreement to move forward

Step 6 Determine the prospect's ability to buy

Step 7a Negotiate for access to power

At the end of Step 4, you concluded the 9 Block Vision Processing Model by summarizing the created or reengineered buying vision. You are now ready to proceed to Step 5.

STEP 5: GAIN AGREEMENT TO MOVE FORWARD

This is a simple and straightforward step to accomplish. It does, however, serve as an important segue between vision processing and determining the prospect's ability to buy.

⇨ *What is the buyer's perspective during this step?*

The buyer is deciding about moving forward and whether he or she is prepared to promote this new idea to power.

⇦ *What are the activities that help you create alignment with the buyer at this step?*

You should ask questions that help gauge the buyer's desire to move forward. I suggest that you choose one of two options, as demonstrated by the following examples:

"I am reasonably sure that we can provide you with those capabilities. I want to check some things with my resources. If they confirm what we just discussed, will you further evaluate us?"
[*Get buyer's agreement.*]

or

"I'm confident that we can provide you with those capabilities, and I would like the opportunity to prove it to you. Would you give me that opportunity?"
[*Get buyer's agreement.*]

Although the difference between the two examples is slight, there are times when you might prefer the tone of one over the other.

Option 1 is less committal. You might use this approach in the following situations:

- When you are sure you are only at a sponsor level and you don't want to overcommit to someone who can't make a purchasing decision

- When you are not sure whether you can deliver the total vision and need to check with your resources

- When you are confident of your capabilities but want to take a more consultative approach by not having the answer so quickly

Option 2 is more committal. You might use this approach in the following situations:

- When you are sure you are at the power sponsor level and you want to gain the confidence of the decision maker quickly

- When you are in a reengineering scenario and have a small window of time to respond to the established requirements

- When you are confident of your capabilities and do not want to prolong the sell cycle

Assuming that the buyer has not volunteered access to power, move on to Step 6.

⇨ *What is the buyer's perspective during this step?*

The buyer is deciding whether or not to reveal the identity of the power sponsor.

⇨ *What are the activities that help you create alignment with the buyer at this step?*

You should ask questions that help draw out the identity of the power sponsor. One way of doing this is to ask a question that seeks to understand the buyer's process, as demonstrated by the following example:

> "Let's say you become convinced that it really is possible for you to [*repeat buying vision*] and you want to go forward. What do you do then? Who else is involved?"

When you ask, "Who else is involved?" you are trying to uncover the buying process and find out who will have the most impact on the purchasing decision. This question tests the person's ability to fulfill the role of either a sponsor or a power sponsor.

In this chapter, we will look at the scenario in which the buyer indicates willingness to play the role of a sponsor.

Sponsor Checklist

This buyer will

❒ Provide information about the organization and project

❐ Actively promote the opportunity and sell internally for you

❐ *Not* make the buying decision—although he or she may influence it

❐ Provide you access to power

Once the potential sponsor reveals the identity of power, you should proceed to the next step of the Strategic Alignment Prompter.

STEP 7A: BARGAIN FOR ACCESS TO POWER

❐   IF NECESSARY, NEGOTIATE AND STRIKE A BARGAIN FOR ACCESS TO POWER—QUID PRO QUO.

⇨   *What is the buyer's perspective during this step?*

How much pain the buyer is in and how well you have been able to diagnose the pain and create a vision will determine the buyer's frame of mind. Generally, if the buyer's pain is at a high level and if the buyer likes what he or she has heard, the buyer is usually very willing to provide access to power. On the other hand, the buyer may need to be thoroughly convinced that the prescribed solution can work before providing access.

⇦   *What are the activities that help you create alignment with the buyer at this step?*

You should ask to meet with power (e.g., Could we get on his or her calendar?). If this is denied, you should strike a bargain for access to power. This is demonstrated by the following example:

"It may be premature at this point, but let me suggest this, I'm not yet sure of the best way for us to prove these capabilities to you. I first want to consult with my resources. Whichever method we end up using [*to prove these capabilities*], it will take some of my company's resources. I'm willing to make that commitment today. If through that effort we succeed in proving to you that you will be able to [*repeat buying vision*], at that point, will you then introduce me to [*power person*], is that fair? [*Get buyer's agreement and end call.*]"

Keep in mind that the phraseology used in this example may not be applicable to your industry or environment. However, let me encourage you to adapt the concept and put it into words and terminology that do apply. Ultimately you want a fair exchange or a quid pro quo with the buyer.

"Is that fair?" can be a powerful question to ask a buyer. It tends to analyze how reasonable the buyer is. You are asking the buyer to introduce you to power *only* if he or she is convinced that the capabilities you have described will address the buying vision. I believe most people would indeed see that as a fair bargain.

At this point, most buyers who have a vision of how to solve a pain will agree to the bargain. If for some reason a buyer does not agree to the bargain, you should do one of three things

- Find another sponsor on your own
- Ask the buyer for a contact name who the buyer feels would sponsor you
- Tactfully disengage

☐ END THE CALL AND POSITION THE FOLLOW-UP SPONSOR LETTER

If the buyer agrees to the bargain, you should end the call by suggesting next steps that include a recap of the information uncovered in the call and the specific way you intend to fulfill your end of the bargain. This is demonstrated by the following example:

"Thank you for your time. I am going to consult with my resources. I will then write you a letter/e-mail confirming my understanding of your situation. In that letter, I will suggest a specific way for us to prove these capabilities to you. You should receive that letter/e-mail shortly."

There are six key components in the body of a well-written Sponsor Letter. I've highlighted the six items in the sample that follows. Let's see how well you can identify the six elements.

EXERCISE: DETERMINE SPONSOR LETTER COMPONENTS, PART I

Activities

- Review the sample Sponsor Letter for vision creation that follows.

- Determine which key component each of the six numbered and underlined sections found in the sample Sponsor Letter represents.

- Record the number corresponding to each of the key components.

Key Components	Number (1 to 6)
Capabilities needed (buying vision)	_____
Suggested proof step	_____
Pain	_____
Recall bargain for access to power	_____
Reasons for pain	_____
Agreement to explore further	_____

Answers: Capabilities needed (buying vision), 3; suggested proof step, 6; pain, 1; recall bargain for access to power, 5; reasons for pain, 2; agreement to explore further, 4.

Sample Sponsor Letter (e-mail) for Vision Creation

Dear Steve,

Thank you for your interest in our company. The purpose of this letter is to summarize my understanding of our meeting and our action plan.

We discussed the following:

❶ <u>Your primary critical issue is missing new account revenue targets by $10 million.</u>

❷ <u>Reasons you are missing your new account revenue targets</u>:
- Your salespeople spend too much time handling repeat business in existing accounts instead of developing new customers.
- Salespeople are spending too much time answering FAQs from customers.
- Prospects are unaware of promotions.
- Your salespeople are not asking existing customers to refer potential new business.

❸ <u>Capabilities you said you needed</u>:
- Whenever wanting to order, customers need to be able to view available stock, place their order, and have it allocated and confirmed using the Internet.
- When customers have questions, they need to be able to click on an FAQ menu on your Web site or select an "I need help" button to be connected to the appropriate person in your company.
- When offering new promotions, your salespeople need to be able to create personalized messages and broadcast them to all their customers via e-mail.
- Customers need to be prompted to submit referrals for new business when they place an order on your Web site.

You said that if you had these capabilities, your salespeople would have the time to develop new customers, allowing you to achieve your new account revenue targets.

Our next steps: **❹** <u>You agreed to move forward with our company,</u> and you said that if **❺** <u>we succeed in proving that we can give you these capabilities, you will introduce me to Jim Smith, your Vice President of Finance.</u> You mentioned that Jim is not happy with the revenue shortfall and its impact on profits.

❻ <u>I would like to propose that we arrange a meeting with another sales executive who has implemented an e-commerce application with our help.</u> I am confident that you will like what you see and will introduce our company to the rest of your organization. I'll call you Monday to discuss it further.

Sincerely,

Bill Hart

Sponsor Letter (or e-mail) for Vision Creation

Overview

The Sponsor Letter for vision creation is a letter or e-mail sent to the prospective buyer that documents and confirms a buying vision that you created. The letter further confirms the buyer's intention to introduce you to the potential power sponsor. In essence, the Sponsor Letter is confirmation of the conversation you had.

Where/How Used

The Sponsor Letter for vision creation contains six key elements from discussions with the sponsor, summarized in your words. The elements are

1. Pain

2. Reasons for pain

3. Capabilities needed (buying vision)

4. Agreement to explore further

5. Bargain for access to power

6. Suggested proof step—what you offered in return for access to power

What You Should Achieve

- A mutual understanding of what was discussed during the vision creation conversation. If the potential sponsor does not agree with the elements of the letter, you are able to find this out before proceeding.

- The sponsor perceives you as thorough, organized, and professional.

- Access to power.

Input Required
To create the Sponsor Letter, you need details on the sponsor's pain, the reasons for the pain, the buying vision created, and options to offer as proof.

The Sponsor Letter written to confirm a conversation in which vision creation took place is slightly different from the one used to confirm a conversation in which vision reengineering occurred.

EXERCISE: DETERMINE SPONSOR LETTER COMPONENTS, PART II

Activities

- Review the sample Sponsor Letter for vision reengineering that follows.

- Determine which key component each of the six numbered and underlined sections found in the sample Sponsor Letter for vision reengineering represents.

- Record the number corresponding to each of the key components.

Key Components	Number (1 to 6)
Prospect's original vision	_____
Organizational impact and access to power	_____
Salesperson's additional capabilities	_____
Expanded buying vision	_____
Proof requirement of all vendors	_____
Reasons and resulting pain	_____

Answers: Prospect's original vision, 1; Organizational impact and access to power, 5; Salesperson's additional capabilities, 2; Expanded buying vision, 3; Proof requirement of all vendors, 6; Reasons and resulting pain, 4.

Sample Sponsor Letter (e-mail) for Vision Reengineering

Dear Steve,

Thank you for your interest in our company. The purpose of this letter is to summarize my understanding of our meeting and our action plan.

❶ <u>Capabilities you said you needed:</u> When you called, you told me that you were looking for a way to allow your customers to order from you via the Internet. In our discussion, you stated more specifically that you wanted your customers, when they wanted to order, to be able to view available stock, place their order, and have it allocated and confirmed, all on the Internet. **❷** <u>As our discussion progressed, you told me you also wanted a way that,</u> when a question presented itself, a customer could select an "I need help" button and speak to someone in your sales department, and when offering new promotions, your salespeople could create personalized messages and broadcast them to all their customers via e-mail and when customers are ordering from your Web site.

❸ <u>You said that if you had these capabilities in addition to customer enabled ordering, your salespeople would have the time to develop new name customers, allowing you to achieve your new account sales targets.</u>

❹ <u>Reasons for needing a new system:</u>
- Your salespeople spend too much time handling repeat business in existing accounts.
- Salespeople spend too much time answering frequently asked questions from customers.
- Prospects are unaware of your promotions.
- Salespeople fail to ask customers for referrals or leads.

<u>This has resulted in new account sales revenues of $10 million below target.</u>

Our next steps: **❺** <u>You mentioned that your current situation directly impacts Donna Moore, your COO, and Jim Smith, your Vice President of Finance.</u> You will be scheduling a meeting with them so that we can discuss the organizational impact of this issue. At that meeting, we can mutually agree on the appropriate next steps. **❻** As we discussed, <u>I will be required to provide proof that we can give you these capabilities, and you will require that same proof from all other potential vendors.</u>

I am available for our next meeting this coming Tuesday and Wednesday from 1 to 5 p.m. I will call you Monday morning to schedule the appointment; it should take about 45 minutes.

Sincerely,

Bill Hart

EXERCISE: CREATE A SPONSOR LETTER FOR YOUR OPPORTUNITY

Activities

- Use the templates that follow.

- Write a Sponsor Letter that could be sent to the buyer sponsoring you within your opportunity.

- Select either the Vision Creation or Vision Reengineering Sponsor Letter template based on the origin of your opportunity.

Note: The six key components of the Sponsor Letter will require that you have engaged with a sponsor in a vision processing conversation and agreed upon the next steps.

Sponsor Letter (or e-mail) for Vision Creation Template

Dear _____ [*sponsor's name*],

Thank you for your interest in _____ [*your company*]. The purpose of this letter is to summarize my understanding of our meeting and our action plan.

We discussed the following:

Your primary critical issue is _____.

Reasons you are having this critical business issue are

Reason A: _____

Reason B: _____

Reason C: _____

Capabilities you said you needed to resolve this situation are

Capability A: _____

Capability B: _____

Capability C: _____

Our next steps:

You agreed to move forward with our company, and you said that if we succeed in proving we can give you these capabilities, you will introduce me to _____ [*power sponsor name and title*]. You mentioned that *he/she* is not happy with the impact that [*your critical business issue*] is having upon *his/her* ability to _____.

I would like to propose that _____
_____

[*describe the proof step needed if it is part of a bargain for access to power*].

I am confident that you will like what you see and will introduce our company to the rest of your organization. I'll call you on _____ to discuss it further.

Sincerely,

_____

Sponsor Letter (or e-mail) for Vision Reengineering Template

Dear _____ [*sponsor's name*],

Thank you for your interest in _____ [*your company*]. The purpose of this letter is to summarize my understanding of our meeting and our action plan.

Capabilities you said you needed: When we began our conversation, you were looking for the ability to [*describe original capabilities needed*]:
Capability A: _____,

As our conversation progressed, you also told me you needed a way to [*describe additional capabilities needed*]
Capability B: _____
Capability C: _____
Capability D: _____

You said that if you had these capabilities, you could better address your critical business issue of _____.

Reasons you are having this critical business issue are

Reason A: _____,
Reason B: _____,
Reason C: _____,
Reason D: _____.

Our next steps:

You agreed to move forward with our company, and you said that if we succeed in proving that we can give you these capabilities, you will introduce me to _____ [*power sponsor name and title*]. You mentioned that *he/she* is not happy with the impact that [*your critical business issue*] is having upon *his/her* ability to _____.

At that meeting we can mutually agree on appropriate next steps. As we discussed, I will be required to provide proof that we can give you these capabilities, and you will require that proof of all other potential consultants. I look forward to our next meeting on _____.

Sincerely,

_____

Summary

Gaining access to power is a critical step in winning a sales opportunity. This is not always easy to do, so effective bargaining is important because it will allow you to gain access that otherwise you might not be able to gain. The key to the bargain is offering a fair exchange of your time and resources for access to power.

CHAPTER 10

HOW TO CONTROL THE BUYING PROCESS

Why is controlling the buying process so important?

Ultimately, it's all about winning—if you control or exert influence over the buying process, you should win.

In the last chapter, I reviewed the successful sales formula Pain × Power × Vision × Value × Control = Successful Sale in order to stress the importance of gaining access to power. In this chapter, I'll describe the sales activities that should occur after you gain access to power. These activities will help you to establish control of the buying process. The focus of this chapter will be on the last element of the successful sales formula: control.

Solution Selling defines control in multiple ways, including

1. Leading the prospect in the direction you want her or him to go

2. Being able to control the buying process, *not* the buyer

3. Letting the buyer have *your* way.

Control, in essence, is the ability to influence and direct the buying process in a consultative manner without manipulating the buyer.

In this chapter, you'll find principles, exercises, and job aids that will help you to exercise control over the buying process. Those Solution Selling job aids are

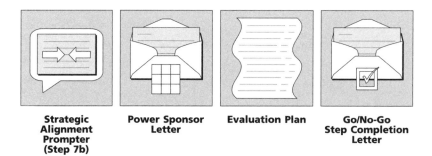

| Strategic Alignment Prompter (Step 7b) | Power Sponsor Letter | Evaluation Plan | Go/No-Go Step Completion Letter |

Making the Transition from a Sponsor to a Power Sponsor

The time period between your meeting with a sponsor and your meeting with a power sponsor can be as short as a few minutes or as long as days, weeks, or even months, depending upon the situation. No matter what the length of time is, after you have proved yourself to the sponsor, under the terms of the bargain that was agreed to, the sponsor is obligated to provide you with access to power.

Power Sponsor Checklist

This buyer

❐ Has enough influence or authority (regardless of title) to make a purchasing decision happen if he or she wants to, even if the purchase is unbudgeted

❐ Will take you anywhere in the organization that's needed

❐ Will commit to a negotiated set of steps that leads to a buying decision

Once you are at power, you virtually start the process over again. You will have to determine the pains of the power-level person and create a vision that matches your unique capabilities, just as you did previously with the sponsor. I recommend that you engage in the same sales activities described in the first six steps of the Strategic Alignment Prompter introduced in Chapter 5. The key difference is that you are now dealing with a person who has the influence or authority to make buying decisions. Because of this person's influence and authority, you want to know as much as possible about how she or he buys things and what the evaluation criteria might be. See Step 7b of the Strategic Alignment Prompter that follows for more details.

STEP 7B: QUALIFY THE BUYING PROCESS WITH POWER
⇨ *What is the buyer's perspective during this step?*

The buyer is deciding if he or she is serious enough about the opportunity to disclose the buying process.

⇦ *What are the activities that help you create alignment with the buyer at this step?*

You should ask questions that

- Remove all ambiguity from the buyer's evaluation criteria

- Introduce ideas that you feel will bias the evaluation process in your favor

As you read and review these questions, keep in mind that your selling situation may be less complex than this example. Scale your approach as required for your selling environment.

❏ **ASK OPEN QUESTION, SET UP GROUND RULES FOR PROPOSAL**

An example of an open question that invites the power sponsor to describe how he or she wants to evaluate the selling organization and the solution is included here. Examples of additional questions that help to uncover the evaluation process follow.

"How would you like to evaluate us?" [*Write down each request as you repeat it. Do not agree or disagree.*]

"If we get to a point where we might want to do business, will there be a legal review? a technical review? an administrative approval?"

"Will you want a proposal from me? [*Get buyer's agreement.*] As part of that proposal, will you also want a value analysis?"

Once you attempt to set up the ground rules for the proposal by asking, "How would you like to evaluate us?" you should take notes in order to record the buyer's requests. It is important that you do not agree or disagree with any of the power sponsor's requests. Why do I suggest that? The simple answer is that now is not the time for you to discuss the specifics of what you think is or is not a reasonable request. The focus could dangerously shift from this wonderful buying vision and value that the prospect is envisioning receiving to "this one little thing" that you might not do. There is a better time to deal with the handling of the power sponsor's requests. That takes shape in the form of something called an Evaluation Plan. The Evaluation Plan will help to define the sell cycle from that point forward. We will look at that shortly.

I recommend that, as part of determining the buying process, you try to uncover all the customer approvals needed. That's why you should ask a question such as, "If we get to a point where we might want to do business, will there be legal, technical, or administrative approvals?" The thought is not to ask questions that are going to add additional time and effort to the project, but rather to be aware of the buyer's process now rather than ignore it and have surprises later.

I recommend asking buyers, "Will you want a proposal from me?" You ask this question because it gives you the chance to define a proposal on your own terms and to control when and under what circumstances you will provide it.

☐ STATE "NO NEW INFORMATION" AND PRE-PROPOSAL REVIEW THEMES

The sample statements that follow suggest a review of the proposal before the final delivery.

"When you ask me to prepare a proposal, I want you to know that it will contain no new information. It will simply document and confirm the business arrangements we will have discussed up to that point.
[*Get buyer's agreement.*]

I suggest that (if we get that far) I come out a week in advance of our delivery of the final proposal with a rough draft. We call this a pre-proposal review. There are two advantages to this approach. The advantage to you is there will be no surprises in the final proposal; the advantage to me is that I can prepare it correctly the first time."
[*Get buyer's agreement and end call.*]

This portion of Step 7b defines the proposal process and establishes an important meeting to be held prior to delivery of the final proposal. The question invites the buyer to agree to the proposal definition.

☐ END THE CALL AND POSITION A POWER SPONSOR LETTER WITH AN EVALUATION PLAN

Assuming that the buyer agreed to the proposal definition, you should end the call and suggest next steps. This is demonstrated by the following example.

"Thank you for your time. I am going to take this list back with me. I will then make an initial attempt to put together a plan for you to evaluate our [*company/ products/services*]. You should receive the draft plan in a day or so. I will call you to discuss it."

Now that we're at power, we're willing to commit resources to an evaluation, and we make that suggestion as we close the call. We then confirm our understanding with a Power Sponsor Letter and also attach a suggested Evaluation Plan.

Power Sponsor Letter (or e-mail)

Overview

The Power Sponsor Letter is a letter or e-mail you send that documents and confirms a buying vision that you helped create with a potential power sponsor. The Power Sponsor Letter is similar to the Sponsor Letter in both style and content, with the exception that an Evaluation Plan is attached with the Power Sponsor Letter. In essence, the Power Sponsor Letter is a confirmation of the conversation had during vision processing.

Where/How Used

The Power Sponsor Letter contains six key elements from discussions with the power sponsor, summarized in your words. Those elements are

1. Pain

2. Reasons for pain

3. Capabilities needed (buying vision)

4. Organizational impact

5. Agreement to explore further

6. Evaluation Plan

What You Should Achieve

- A mutual understanding of what was discussed during the vision processing conversation. If the potential power sponsor does not agree with the elements of the letter, it helps if you find that out before proceeding so that corrective actions can be taken.

- The power sponsor perceives you as thorough, organized, and professional.

Input Required

To create the Power Sponsor Letter, you need specific details on the power sponsor's pain, the reasons for the pain, and the buying vision created, and you need to be able to articulate the impact of the power sponsor's pain on others in the organization.

Power Sponsor Letter (or e-mail) Example

Dear Jim,

Thank you for meeting with Steve Jones and me earlier today. I believe the time was well spent for both of us.

We discussed the following:

Your primary critical issue is declining profits as a result of the revenue shortfall. You said you were about $8 million below plan.

Reasons for declining profits:
- Missing new account revenue targets
- Rising operational costs
- Increasing credit write-offs

Capabilities you said you needed:
- When visiting your Web site, your customers could place and confirm orders via the Internet, get questions answered through a FAQ menu, be notified of promotions, and be prompted to submit referrals.
- For customers to be able to click on a FAQ Web menu to get their answers and require a CSR only for extraordinary situations.
- Prior to accepting an order, your Web site could alert your customer to outstanding credit issues needing to be resolved, with the ability to speak to someone in your accounting department.

You said that if you had these capabilities, Steve could meet his revenue targets, Donna Moore could reduce operating expenses, your controller could reduce the average age of his receivables, and you would be able to increase profits by at least $4.5 million.

Our next steps:

When I told you I was confident that our company could help you integrate an e-commerce application with your existing internal accounting and inventory systems, you agreed to commit the resources needed to evaluate our ability to do so. Based on my knowledge to date, I am attaching a suggested evaluation plan for your further exploration of our company. Look it over with Steve, and I will call you on February 7 to get your thoughts.

Sincerely,
Bill Hart

Attachment:
Draft Evaluation Plan

Evaluation Plan

Overview

The Evaluation Plan is a job aid used in conjunction with the Power Sponsor Letter. It outlines the suggested steps that you want to be followed.

Where/How Used

The Evaluation Plan captures events that you and power sponsors can agree upon. You assign dates to each event with the thought of closing the sale on an agreed-upon date. This helps to control and shorten sales cycles. The Evaluation Plan should be a mutually owned project plan.

What You Should Achieve

The Evaluation Plan should help you maintain control of the buying process by documenting all events that will take place during the course of the sale and the sequence in which those events will take place. By managing this plan with a buyer, you can predict when resources will be needed and anticipate potential hurdles to closure of the sale. Changes to the draft plan made by power sponsors are an indication of ownership and "buy-in" to the approach.

Input Required

To create an Evaluation Plan, you need to know the buyer's criteria for buying and to have an understanding of your company's recommended approach for evaluation. Some other things that you should consider include

- Month-end, quarter-end, year-end, and other periodic events

- Whether or not any of the events should be billable

- The time required to accomplish each event

- Resources needed to execute the events in the plan

Six Evaluation Plan Tips

Request additional interviews with customer individuals as early as possible in the sequence of events—as the first step, if possible. This not only allows you to attempt to expand the scope of the opportunity by meeting with other beneficiaries from the Pain Chain, but also tests both the buyer's sponsorship and his or her seriousness about proceeding.

Another early step should be a summarization of the findings from all the customer individuals interviewed. You should gain agreement on the content of the draft Evaluation Plan before proceeding further because the events that follow can require investment of time, resources, and money by both parties.

Before quoting a price to the buyer and creating a value justification, you should attempt to understand and gain acceptance of all the capabilities needed by the buyer. This might also include additional capabilities such as implementation and customer support services.

When you conduct a value analysis, it is an opportune time to establish success criteria. Doing so at this point seems natural because the criteria can be very similar to the benefits described and agreed upon in a value analysis.

Include buyer approvals (i.e., legal, technical, and administrative approvals) early in the sequence of events, instead of letting them become hurdles near the end of the sales process.

Suggest a pre-proposal review so that the buyer will see no surprises in the final proposal. The pre-proposal review should be scheduled as the event right before the delivery of the final proposal.

By following these tips, you can determine the optimal sequence of events and produce an effective Evaluation Plan. Before I show you an example of an Evaluation Plan, however, I'd like you to practice the process of constructing one.

EXERCISE: BUILDING AN EVALUATION PLAN

Activities

- Read the short scenario provided.

- Review the six Evaluation Plan tips.

- Resequence the list of events that follow in the optimal order in which they should appear in order to create the most effective Evaluation Plan.

Note: A few events have already been placed within the "Resequenced Events" column to get you started.

Scenario

The salesperson, Bill Hart, has met with both the sponsor (Steve Jones, Vice President of Sales) and the power sponsor (Jim Smith, Vice President of Finance). They both have a distinct buying vision of how they could address their pains, and they have suggested that they would like to have two key proof sessions:

1. To prove the operational capabilities to the key members of the management team after the plan is accepted.

2. To review the likely return on their investment through a detailed value analysis before involving legal.

They also suggested that a visit to Bill Hart's headquarters in order to meet with Bill's extended team would be something they would like to do. They suggested doing this right before the first review of the proposal.

Bill feels it will be necessary to meet with a few other customer key players who will benefit from the capabilities being recommended and also to perform a detailed survey of current systems before presenting a preliminary solution.

List of Events	Resequenced Events
	1. **Meet with VP Sales (completed)**
	2. **Meet with VP Finance (completed)**
• Present proposal for approval	3.
• *Determine/present value justification*	4.
• Transition kickoff and finalize success criteria	5. Summarize findings to mgmt. and agree to Evaluation Plan
• Visit corporate HQ	6.
• Gain legal approval (terms and conditions)	7.
• Phone interview John Watkins (CIO)	8. Present preliminary solution/design
• *Present preliminary solution/design*	9.
• Measure success criteria	10. Determine/present value justification
• Perform detailed survey of current systems (two days)	11.
• *Summarize findings to top management team and agree to Evaluation Plan*	12.
• Implementation plan approval by IT department	13.
• Phone interview Donna Moore (COO)	14.
• Prove capabilities to top management team	15.
• Agree on preliminary success criteria	16.
• Pre-proposal review meeting	17.
• Send our license agreement to legal	18.

The recommended sequence of these events can be found in the Evaluation Plan example that follows. As you might imagine, the nuances that accompany almost any sales opportunity will cause the sequence of events to vary.

Evaluation Plan Example

[DRAFT]

Event	Week Of	✓	Responsible	Go/No-Go	Billable
Phone interview John Watkins (CIO)	Feb. 14		Us/TGI		
Phone interview Donna Moore (COO)	Feb. 14		Us/TGI		
Summarize findings to top management team and agree to Evaluation Plan	Feb. 21		Us/TGI	*	
Prove capabilities to top management team	Feb. 28		Us	*	
Perform detailed survey of current systems (two days)	Mar. 4		Us		Yes
Present preliminary solution/design	Mar. 11		Us	*	
Implementation plan approval by IT department	Mar. 18		TGI	*	
Determine/present value justification	Mar. 18		Us/TGI	*	
Agree on preliminary success criteria	Mar. 18		Us/TGI		
Send our license agreement to legal	Mar. 18		Us		
Gain legal approval (terms and conditions)	Apr. 4		TGI	*	
Visit corporate HQ	Apr. 11		Us		
Pre-proposal review meeting	Apr. 18		Us		
Present proposal for approval	Apr. 25		Us	*	
Transition kickoff and finalize success criteria	May 10		Us/TGI		
Measure success criteria	Ongoing		TGI		

*Indicates a "go/no-go" mutual decision to be made.

Short sales cycles For shorter sales cycles, the Evaluation Plan may be as simple as a bulleted list included at the end of the Power Sponsor Letter, with only a few steps defined.

One-call close If you attempt to close business in one sales call, the concept of an Evaluation Plan is still applicable. In your conversation with the buyer, you can define a short Evaluation Plan verbally, confirm the steps, and then offer proof immediately.

The more complex the evaluation and buying process, the more elements the Evaluation Plan is likely to contain. The previous example of an Evaluation Plan includes additional recommended columns along with the sequence of events. These columns are:

- *Week Of/Date* This allows you to suggest a time frame for accomplishing all of the events of the Evaluation Plan. Although the column header reads "Week Of," you may find it more appropriate to be more precise by suggesting specific dates.

- ✓ The checkmark column provides a space to indicate that the event has been completed. This becomes useful when the Evaluation Plan is accepted by the buyer, events are executed over time, and a periodic update of the plan is needed.

- *Responsible* This column highlights who is the *primary* owner of the given event. The example lists the name of the buyer (in this case, the fictitious company TGI) and "Us" for the selling organization. It may be appropriate to be more precise and include the names of specific individuals responsible for performing events owned by the buying organization and the selling organization.

- *Go/No-Go* This column is intended to remove pressure from the buyer. The buyer can decide at each asterisk whether or not to continue in the opportunity. This plan gives both the buyer and you control. That is to say, if for some reason continuing the opportunity doesn't make sense, you both have "outs."

- *Billable* This column indicates events that will be fee-based. Including a billable item can be a way to gauge the seriousness of the buyer. It also can be used as a point of negotiation with the buyer. You may refund the fee if the two organizations reach closure; regardless, you have established the value of your services.

If you mark your Evaluation Plan as a draft, it invites the power sponsor to make suggestions and changes. This is a good thing. *If people change it, they own it.* If they say, "It looks perfect," with little enthusiasm, it probably means they haven't really read it.

Once the Evaluation Plan is accepted by the buyer and the events begin to be executed, I recommend sending a simple message to the power sponsor every time one of the go/no-go events is successfully completed.

 ## Go/No-Go Step Completion Letter (or e-mail)

Overview
The Go/No-Go Step Completion Letter is sent to the power sponsor or some other person responsible for executing the steps of the Evaluation Plan. The intent is to confirm that a go/no-go step on the Evaluation Plan has been completed.

Where/How Used
The Go/No-Go Step Completion Letter should be used after completing any event designated as a go/no-go decision on the Evaluation Plan. Other customer individuals involved in the decision-making process can be copied on the letter or e-mail. The completion letter simply advises all parties involved of the steps completed, when the steps were completed, and which step(s) will be taken next.

What You Should Achieve
The Go/No-Go Step Completion Letter can ensure that everyone involved in the opportunity is informed of and in alignment with the progress of the plan's execution. Also, it can serve

as an indicator of additional time and resources that may be necessary.

Input Required

To create the Go/No-Go Step Completion Letter, the development of an Evaluation Plan must be completed, with events or steps, go/no-go decision points, and dates assigned.

Note: The Go/No-Go Step Completion Letter is a simple, yet powerful way to stay in front of the customer on a regular basis. You also may want to include or attach the updated Evaluation Plan showing any changes to the plan as well as the events that have been marked as completed.

Go/No-Go Step Completion Letter (or e-mail) Example

To:	jsmith@tgi.com
cc:	sjones@tgi.com, dmoore@tgi.com, jwatkins@tgi.com, sbrown@tgi.com, kwhite@sellerscompany.com
Subject:	Evaluation Plan—step completion

Jim and team,

I am pleased to report that another milestone has been completed. On February 21 your team approved the evaluation plan. The changes you requested are reflected in the attached copy.

Our next milestone is the week of February 28, when the entire management team is scheduled to visit our client and meet with their senior executives.

Thank you again for your continued support of this project.

Sincerely,
Bill Hart

Attachment:
Updated Evaluation Plan

EXERCISE: CREATE A POWER SPONSOR LETTER FOR YOUR OPPORTUNITY

Activities

- Write a Power Sponsor Letter that could be sent to the buyer acting as the power sponsor within your opportunity.

- Use the Power Sponsor Letter template that follows.

Power Sponsor Letter (e-mail) Template

Dear _____ [*power sponsor's name*],

Thank you for meeting with _____ [*sponsor's name*] and me earlier today. I believe it was time well spent for both of our organizations.

We discussed the following:

Your primary critical issue is _____.

Reasons you are having this critical business issue are

Reason A: _____,
Reason B: _____,
Reason C: _____.

Capabilities you said you needed to resolve this situation are

Capability A: _____
Capability B: _____
Capability C: _____

Our next steps:

When I told you I was confident that our organization can help you to _____ [*describe goal of power sponsor*], you agreed to take a serious look at our ability to do so. Based on my knowledge to date, I am suggesting an evaluation plan for your further exploration of our organization's capabilities. Look over the plan with _____ [*sponsor*] and I will call you on _____ to get your thoughts.

Sincerely,

_____

Attachment:
Draft Evaluation Plan

EXERCISE: CREATE AN EVALUATION PLAN FOR YOUR OPPORTUNITY

Activities

- Draft an Evaluation Plan for your opportunity.

- Use the Evaluation Plan template that follows.

Note: Refer to the Evaluation Plan checklist when building your Evaluation Plan.

Evaluation Plan Checklist

Have you included in your Evaluation Plan events or elements that

- ❏ Suggest that the plan is in a *draft* format?

- ❏ Address the power sponsor's evaluation criteria requests?

- ❏ Include additional customer key players who might need to be interviewed?

- ❏ Promote an early meeting with the customer to summarize findings?

- ❏ Introduce any resources, business partners, or third-party sources that may be used on your behalf to accomplish any given event?

- ❏ Demonstrate value (value justification or analysis, refined value propositions, ROIs, etc.)?

- ❏ Accomplish all necessary proof requirements?

- ❏ Address any legal, technical, financial, and administrative issues?

- ❏ Reflect actions that will strengthen your position?

- ❏ Encourage continuing customer buy-in?

- ❏ Reflect appropriate timing and dates?

- ❏ Position any potential billable activities?

- ❏ Suggest who has primary responsibility for each event?

- ❏ Account for implementation issues, plans, and approaches?

- ❏ Promote the concept of a pre-proposal review?

- ❏ Advocate establishing and measuring success criteria?

Evaluation Plan Template

[DRAFT]					
Event	Week Of	✓	Responsible	Go/No-Go	Billable
*Indicates a "go/no-go" mutual decision to be made.					

Summary

If you exert control over the buying process, you will win—if you don't, you will not.

CHAPTER 11

HOW TO SELL VALUE

Why is selling value important?

Think of all the opportunities for which you've competed during your career. Each one of those opportunities ended in either a win, a loss, or no decision on the part of the prospective buyer. What percentage ended in a win, a loss, and no decision? Write it down:

Win: _____% Loss: _____% No decision: _____% = 100%

Several years ago, I was on the road with a colleague, John Rossmeissl. John loves value justification models, and he enjoys deep conversations about discounted cash flow, internal rates of return, and other financial analysis techniques. During this trip, John articulated the importance of value justification with a simple anecdote that has stuck with me. He said, "Keith, bankers don't make money by sitting on their assets." He chuckled, and then continued, "They make money by investing those assets for a return, and prospective buyers are no different. They are going to invest their money where it makes the most business sense."

The more I thought about that statement, the more I realized that salespeople really do *not* lose because the buyer makes no decision on the current project—they lose because buyers choose to make alternative investments in projects that they feel will give them a better return. The moral of the story is to always provide some level of value justification. You never know when you may be competing against an accounting system, a new fleet of trucks, new office furniture, or some other alternative use of capital.

Note: The building of a value justification model for your business should be done by people with a background and competency in financial justification. However, as a sales professional, it's important that you understand the use of value justifications, even without understanding all the nuances required to build them. One size does not fit all. If your business does not require highly sophisticated value justifications, then you should adapt them to meet the needs of you and your buyers.

In this chapter, you'll find principles, exercises, and job aids that help you to sell with value. Those Solution Selling job aids are

Value Justification Model

Success Criteria

Value Justification Model

I sometimes hear the topic of value justification described by salespeople as a necessary evil. Unlike John, I don't spend my weekends creating intricate value justification models based on complex mathematical formulas—I'm not built that way, and most salespeople aren't either.

But I do know that when a salesperson asks a buyer to spend a significant amount of money, someone in the buying organization has to justify the decision. If you know this is going to happen, then you should lead that effort.

THE BEST RELATIONSHIPS ARE BASED ON VALUE

Of course, having a friendly relationship with a customer makes doing business much more pleasant. However, often a salesperson comes to rely on the development of a *personal* relationship rather than on the value that the customer receives.

Imagine this scenario: Your long-time contact for your biggest account leaves, retires, or is let go from the company. How would you respond if the Chief Financial Officer then asked, "What value has my organization received from you and your organization?"

This would be a difficult question unless you had constantly demonstrated, delivered, and quantified the value over the life of the relationship. Therefore, the best business relationships are always based and sustained on value.

The Value Cycle

Too many salespeople wait too long to convince buyers that their solutions provide value. As a result, they usually end up making too many concessions, resulting in lower revenues and profits. A better way is to make value an integral part of the entire sales process. You should lead with value, verify the value that you can deliver, justify the value to help close the sale, and measure the value received by the customer.

In Chapter 4, I discussed how to *lead* with Value Propositions to stimulate interest. This is accomplished by extrapolating the value that an existing client is receiving, and projecting the value that a prospective buyer might obtain if the buyer were able to achieve the same or similar results.

In Chapter 6, I discussed how to use the 9 Block Vision Processing Model to diagnose a buyer's pain. Proper diagnosis allows you to ask quantifying "drill-down" questions that help you verify or refine the initial assumptions made when delivering the Value Proposition. During this verification stage, the initial Value Proposition can be expanded as pains of other individuals in the buying organization are uncovered.

In this chapter, I'll further discuss how getting the buyer to agree to the potential benefits and estimated investment will enable you to put together a more formalized statement of value (Value Justification Model) that helps *close* opportunities.

Additionally, I'll discuss how to establish success criteria for the project so that the value can be *measured* after implementation.

The changing role of value in selling (the *value cycle*) is illustrated in the following diagram:

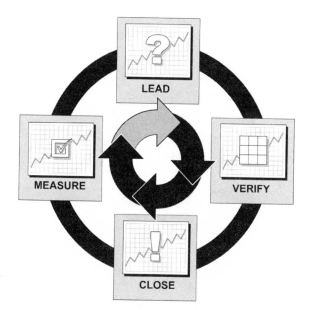

117

K.shoull@okflondoc.edu
Kathy

Value Justification Model

Overview

A Value Justification Model is used to document and present the projected benefits associated with the use of your products and services after implementation. The projected, quantifiable benefits are presented in relation to the total investment being made by the buying organization.

Where/How Used

A Value Justification Model is usually presented during the proof phase of a selling cycle. It provides a detailed breakdown of the projected benefits (profit and revenue increases and cost decreases) to the buyer's organization. The schedule of investments (one-time and ongoing) to be made by the buyer is also explained.

Note: Success in using Value Justification Models is recognized when the metrics of the analysis are derived from and owned by the buyer. These metrics are usually derived from your vision processing conversations with the buyers.

What You Should Achieve

Using a Value Justification Model will clearly define the potential value to be received by both you and the buyer. This provides you with logical reasons to give fewer concessions during negotiations. It also gives the buyer a compelling reason to take action.

Input Required

Completion of a Value Justification Model requires you to know the estimated customer investment for the entire project, the projected benefits associated with the use of the implemented offerings, and a reasonable prediction of when benefits can begin to be realized.

Note: Exercise caution when using the term *ROI* (return on investment), since most buyers have their own definition of what that means.

Value Justification Model Example

Phased over Time (in 000s)

	Q1	Q2	Q3	Q4
BENEFITS				
Increased profit (1) from increased revenue	0.0	293.33	586.67	880
Reduced cost (2)	0.0	33.33	66.67	100
Avoided cost (2)	13	26	39	52
Quarterly total	13	352.66	692.33	1,032
Cumulative value	13	365.66	1,058	2,090
INVESTMENTS				
One-time investment	(641)	(271)	0	0
Ongoing investment	(97)	(30)	(30)	(30)
Quarterly total	(738)	(301)	(30)	(30)
Cumulative investment	(738)	(1,039)	(1,069)	(1,099)
NET VALUE				
Quarterly total	(725)	51.66	662.33	1,002
Cumulative total	(725)	(673.33)	(11)	991

Sources of data: (1) VP Sales (2) VP Finance	First-year net return: $991,000 Breakeven point Q4 ROI (first year): 90.17%

How to Build Your Value Justification Model

The exercise that follows will serve as a starting point for thinking about constructing your own Value Justification Model. Focus your value justification for now on these five elements:

- What will be measured?
- Who is responsible?
- How much value is possible?
- What capabilities will be needed?
- When will the investment pay for itself?

EXERCISE: BUILD A VALUE JUSTIFICATION MODEL

Activities

- Build your Value Justification Model by answering the five questions:
  - What will be measured?
  - Who is responsible?
  - How much value is possible?
  - What capabilities will be needed?
  - When will the investment pay for itself?

- Use the Value Justification Model Worksheet that follows to capture your final work.

Notes

- You may find it useful to brainstorm and work through these questions on a scrap sheet of paper or in the margins of this fieldbook in order to arrive at your final input to the model.

- Refer to the helpful hints located after the worksheet

Value Justification Model Worksheet
Phased over Time (in 000s)

	Q1	Q2	Q3	Q4
BENEFITS				
Increased profit from increased revenue				
Reduced cost				
Avoided cost				
Quarterly total				
Cumulative value				
INVESTMENTS				
One-time investment				
Ongoing investment				
Quarterly total				
Cumulative investment				
NET VALUE				
Quarterly total				
Cumulative total				

Sources of data:	First-year net return: $_____
	Breakeven point: Q_____
	ROI (first year): _____%

Helpful hints:

- Identify negative metrics by enclosing them in parentheses—e.g., negative $641 is written (641).

- The quarterly totals and cumulative value or investment will be the same in Q1.

- Add the cumulative value or investment for one quarter to the total for the next quarter to calculate the cumulative value or investment for that next quarter.

- The cumulative total for the net value of Q4 is known as the *first year net return*.

- The quarter in which the breakeven point occurs can be identified when the net value's cumulative total turns from a negative to a positive metric.

- When presenting a value justification that has early investments (mostly in Q1) and a longer ramp-up time to benefits, it may be necessary to show the return on investment analysis beyond one year (i.e., for two to three years).

If you refer to the Evaluation Plan example in Chapter 10, you'll notice that "determine/present value justification" and "agree on preliminary success criteria" are suggested as events that will take place on the same day. Why? When the prospective buyer agrees to the value justification, it is an ideal time to agree upon success criteria because the baseline for the criteria has been established.

Success Criteria

Overview

Success Criteria establish the baseline metrics for measuring the effectiveness and value of your capabilities in the prospective buyer's organization.

Where/How Used

Success Criteria should be mutually defined and agreed upon during the evaluation process. After delivery of your solution to the customer, you should measure the Success Criteria on an ongoing basis and report the results to the customer.

What You Should Achieve

- Higher levels of customer satisfaction as the customer understands the value of the solutions you have provided

- Credibility for you and your company

- Additional business from future projects

Input Required

To create the initial Success Criteria, the buying and selling organizations should agree on the current baseline metrics to be measured. They also should determine how often each metric will be measured (e.g., monthly, quarterly, or biannually).

Note: You should ensure that the Success Criteria can be attributed to your offerings. Success Criteria that are too broad may allow outside factors to affect the results.

Success Criteria Example

Success Criteria	Baseline	Q1	Q2	Q3	Q4
Average # of new accounts per rep per quarter (1)	2.5				
Web site orders placed per customer (1)	0%				
Number of referrals per quarter (1)	7.5				
Credit write-offs per quarter (2)	$200K				
Number of customer service reps (2)	18				
Sources of data: (1) VP Sales (2) VP Finance					

EXERCISE: DETERMINING YOUR SUCCESS CRITERIA

Activities

- Develop a list of reasonable success criteria that you could present to your customer for approval.
  - Record the baseline metric for each criterion.

> ○ Refer to "Exercise: Build Your Value Justification" to help you determine specific criteria and the baseline for each.
>
> ○ Use the Success Criteria template that follows to record your work.
>
> **Note:** You will not need to fill out the quarterly information until you actually start to measure the criteria.

Success Criteria Template

Success Criteria	Baseline	Q1	Q2	Q3	Q4
Sources of data:					

Summary

Make value an integral part of the entire sales process. You should lead with value, verify the value you can deliver, justify the value to help close the sale, and measure the value received by your customer on an ongoing basis.

CHAPTER 12

HOW TO REACH FINAL AGREEMENT

What are the keys to effectively reaching final agreement with buyers?

During my years of selling and managing salespeople, I've come to the conclusion that there are three principles that you should embrace if you are to effectively reach final agreement with buyers. They are

- Correctly define what *closing* is and is not.
- Create an atmosphere of "win-win" for both organizations.
- Prepare in order to reach final agreement.

When I mention these to customers, I sometimes can tell what they're thinking: "Keith, we agree that those are nice, honorable principles, but they are hard to adhere to when you've got the everyday pressure of making revenue and profit numbers."

It would be wonderful if salespeople could win all their opportunities—with high margins—and do so quickly, so that they can pursue their next opportunity. However, if salespeople focus on closing as soon as possible, then they aren't enabling their buyers to progress naturally through the buying process. Also, if they approach opportunities thinking only, "What is in this for me?" then they are creating an atmosphere of "win-lose." Premature and greedy attempts at closing make prospective buyers feel uncomfortable and manipulated.

In this chapter, you'll find exercises and a job aid that support these three principles that help you reach final agreement with buyers. The primary Solution Selling job aid that helps accomplish this is

Negotiating Worksheet

Defining "Closing"

The word *close* can be tricky to define. It is a term that many salespeople define as "the big event at the end of the sale." I prefer to define closing in two distinct ways: throughout the sell cycle and at the end of the sell cycle.

During a sell cycle, closing is a series of multiple conclusions or "mini-closes." Nowhere should that be more obvious than in the adherence to a defined sales process and the execution of an Evaluation Plan.

At the *end* of a buying process, closing is the natural evolution of the process. In other words, you shouldn't really have to close. You should create an environment and an opportunity where the prospective buyer wants to start doing business with you.

BASIC PRINCIPLE

DON'T CLOSE
BEFORE IT'S CLOSABLE

If you can think of a reason why your opportunity is not ready to close, you can rest assured that the buyer has thought of it, too. One of the definitions of closing that I mentioned previously is the "natural evolution of the process." I encourage salespeople to remind their managers of this definition if they are ever pressured to adopt the "close early and often" mentality. Rather, they should explain where they are in the buyer's process, which should illustrate why the sale is not yet closable. Remember, buyers have a buying process that they must go through in order to reach closure. Your job is to help the buyer through that process.

As a matter of fact, there are five questions that should be answered when responding to the bigger question, "Is this opportunity closable today?"

Is the Opportunity Closable Checklist

❏ Have you met with the customer individual who has the power to buy?

❏ Has the payback from the value justification been agreed upon?

❏ Have all approvals (e.g., legal, technical, or administrative) been given?

❏ Has the Evaluation Plan been completed?

❏ Does the buyer know the entire investment for the project?

Answering yes to these questions puts you in a position not only to close, but also to prepare effectively for final negotiations.

Another important factor in preparing for final negotiations is to be prepared to walk away from the opportunity if the buyer is asking for too much.

BASIC PRINCIPLE	IF YOU'RE NOT READY TO WALK, YOU'RE NOT READY TO SELL

If you are not ready to walk away from an opportunity, then you probably are not in a position to reach final agreement effectively either.

The principle here is simple, but the ability to adhere to it is not. If you don't know the value that your solution provides to the prospective buyer, you are at a distinct disadvantage. Why? Because you have little, if any, bargaining power.

Create an Atmosphere of Win-Win

Any scenario for win-win should be based on value. We must make sure that we understand the value that the buyer will receive through the use of our solution. Your win will be getting compensated fairly for the value that you deliver to the buyer, not outnegotiating the buyer.

Too often, people say that they want win-win scenarios, but their actions prove otherwise. Instead, I like to think of win-win as the ability to look at a quid pro quo exchange from the buyer's perspective.

How to Prepare for Final Negotiations

1. Be able to answer yes to these questions:
   - Have you met with the customer individual who has the power to buy?
   - Has the payback from the value justification been agreed upon?
   - Have all approvals (legal, technical, administrative, and so on) been given?
   - Has the Evaluation Plan been completed?
   - Does the buyer know the entire investment for the project?

2. Be prepared to engage in quid pro quo.

3. Know what concessions you are looking to accept from the buyer.

4. Know the quantifiable value of the concessions you are prepared to give.

5. Prepare a Negotiating Worksheet.

SALES TIP

Both buyers and salespeople should drop the word *negotiate* from their vocabulary when having discussions with each other. Using the word almost always sends an unconscious signal that there is room to make concessions. When I hear someone say, "Well, we can *negotiate* that later," I know that in his or her own mind, that person is mentally preparing to make concessions.

 Negotiating Worksheet

Overview

The Negotiating Worksheet is used as a prenegotiation preparation tool. It helps you resist requests for concessions that are likely to be made by the buyer.

Where/How Used

The Negotiating Worksheet should be completed prior to discussions to finalize the terms of the sale. It provides guidelines for making stands against buyer concessions. The stands should be based on logical information that you developed during the buying process. Key "stands" may include (in no particular order of importance):

1. *Pain stand* Recall the buyer's pain that is driving the opportunity.

2. *Vision stand* Recall the vision established to address the critical business issue.

3. *Value stand* Recall the quantifiable value associated with addressing the pain.

4. *Plan stand* Recall the Evaluation Plan, indicating the timeline to realize benefits.

What You Should Achieve

- Reduced stress by minimizing the pressure on you to discount your price or give in on terms

- Higher margins

- Fewer concessions

- Improved negotiations

- Better business terms and conditions

Input Required

To create the Negotiating Worksheet, pain must have been uncovered, a buying vision created, a Value Justification Model completed, and an Evaluation Plan with a planned implementation date agreed upon.

Negotiating Worksheet Example

Is it closable today?	✓ Power to buy?	VP Finance	Prepared for:
	✓ Payback agreed to?	VP Fin. / VP Sales	✓ Price?
	✓ L/T/A approvals?		___ Terms?
	✓ Plan completed?		___ Risk?
	✓ Known cost since	4 months	

Stand 1:
PLAN

"Our published plan shows an implementation starting on <u>May 10</u>
[*date*]. Is this issue worth the delay?"

Stand 2:
VALUE

"When we calculated the payback, you said <u>that even with all of the cost included,</u>
<u>it was a higher return than you expected</u>. We agreed that the project would pay
for itself in <u>10</u> months."

Stand 3:
PAIN

"The reason we have spent the last <u>4</u> months together is because <u>you are not</u>
<u>meeting your new account revenue target</u>. That issue will not go away until you
gain these new capabilities."

Stand 4:
VISION

"You told me that you needed a way to <u>enable customers to place their own</u>
<u>orders over the Internet using any standard browser so that your sellers can focus</u>
<u>on selling</u>. As you know, we can provide you that capability."

"The only way I could do something for you is if you could do something for me."
Buyer should ask: *"Like what?"*

Note: Prepare a Give-Get List to help determine the "gets" and "gives" below.

Is it possible for you to: ***move phases 1 and 2 together and take delivery of the***
hardware shipment this quarter?
Is that possible?

SILENCE! ONLY if buyer accepts your condition . . .

If you can ***combine phases 1 and 2,*** then we are prepared to
offer you ***250 hours of implementation consulting,*** which is worth ***$50,000.***
Can we go forward on that basis?

Stands are developed based on logical information developed during the sales process. The *plan stand* incorporates the implementation date found within the Evaluation Plan (Chapter 10). The *value stand* incorporates the suggested time frame for payback found within the Value Justification Model (Chapter 11). The *pain stand* incorporates the Vice President of Sales's pain, confirmed during vision processing, and the *vision stand* incorporates one or multiple capability visions embraced by the Vice President of Sales (Chapters 6 and 8).

Here is an example of a Give-Get List. Notice that the third "get" and the first "give" are the ones found in the Negotiating Worksheet example.

Give-Get List					
Your Priority	**GET**	Value ($)		**GIVE**	Projected Customer Priority
		⇔			
1	Larger (volume) deal	$100K	$200 /hr	Consulting hours	1
2	To become a reference account	?	$20K	Training discount	2
3	Combine phases I and II of project	$20K	$10K	Short-term rental licenses	4
4	Intro TGI business partner with similar needs	?	$10K	Refund on proof of concept already conducted	3
5			$5K	Reduced maintenance cost	5
NO WAY		1	Volume discount on hardware		
		2	Volume discount on software		
		3			

EXERCISE: PREPARE TO REACH FINAL AGREEMENT, PART I

Activities

- Build you own Give-Get List that will be used in conjunction with the Negotiating Worksheet.
  - Think about some final negotiations that you've been part of over your career.
  - Brainstorm a list of concessions that you might like to receive from the buyer ("gets") and a list of concessions that the buyer might like from you ("gives").
  - Prioritize your list of "gets" numerically (1 = highest priority).
  - Analyze the list of "gives" to determine which of them are too valuable to your organization to give away and should be recategorized as "no way." The "gives" that still remain as options for concession should be numerically prioritized from the perspective of the customer (1 = highest projected customer priority).
  - Provide quantifiable value for each concession (if applicable).
  - Use the Give-Get List Worksheet that follows.

Give-Get List Worksheet

Give-Get List						
Your Priority	**GET**	Value ($) ⇔		**GIVE**		Projected Customer Priority
1						
2						
3						
4						
5						
NO WAY		1				
		2				
		3				

EXERCISE: PREPARE TO REACH FINAL AGREEMENT, PART II

Activities

- Develop stands based on the logical information you've developed during your sell cycle and through the use of this fieldbook. If you chose to use the
  - *Plan stand*, then incorporate the implementation date found within your Evaluation Plan (Chapter 10).
  - *Value stand*, then incorporate the time frame for payback found within your Value Justification Model (Chapter 11).
  - *Pain stand*, then incorporate the pain of the power sponsor or the most relevant customer individual. You may want to refer to the Pain Sheet (Chapter

6) or Pain Chain (Chapter 3) that you developed for your opportunity.

○ *Vision stand,* then incorporate one of the capability visions articulated to the power sponsor or the most relevant customer individual. You may want to refer to the Pain Sheet (Chapter 6) that you developed for your opportunity.

■ Incorporate what you consider to be the most reasonable of your "gives" and "gets" from the prior exercise as the last portion of building the Negotiating Worksheet.

■ Use the Negotiating Worksheet template that follows.

Negotiating Worksheet Template

Is it closable today?	___ Power to buy? ___ Payback agreed to? ___ L/T/A approvals? ___ Plan completed? ___ Known cost since	_____ _____ _____	Prepared for: ___ Price? ___ Terms? ___ Risk?

Stand 1:
PLAN

"Our published plan shows an implementation starting on
_____ [*date*]. Is this issue worth the delay?"

Stand 2:
VALUE

"When we calculated the payback, you said
_____.
We agreed that the project would pay for itself in ___ months."

Stand 3:
PAIN

"The reason we have spent the last ___ months together is
because _____.
That issue will not go away until you gain these new capabilities."

Stand 4:
VISION

"You told me that you needed a way to [*when, who, what*]
_____.
As you know, we can provide you that capability."

"The only way I could do something for you is if you could do something for me."
Buyer should ask: *"Like what?"*

Note: Prepare a Give-Get List to help determine the "gets" and "gives" below.

Is it possible for you to:
_____?
Is that possible?

SILENCE! ONLY if buyer accepts your condition . . .

If you can _____**, then we are**
prepared to
_____**,**
which is worth $_____**.**

Can we go forward on that basis?

Summary

The three keys to effectively reaching final agreement with buyers are

- Viewing *closing* as the natural evolution of the sell cycle instead of trying to "close early and often"
- Creating an atmosphere of "win-win" that fosters success in the current opportunity and future ones
- Preparing in advance for the opportunities in which you want to reach final agreement

CHAPTER 13

HOW TO MEASURE AND LEVERAGE SUCCESS

Why is measuring and leveraging success so important?

Simply put, a solution is an answer to a problem. If a solution was provided, then some measurable result or change should be evident. Real and measurable results to business problems are what businesspeople are searching for.

When you measure success after the sale or after implementation, it sends a strong signal to the buyer that you and your company are interested in the buyer's success. Measuring success provides an opportunity for you and your organization to

- Stay engaged with the customer on a regular basis. During the measurement of success criteria, anything that is not performing up to expectations provides new opportunities.

- Become entrenched in the customer organization, enabling you to identify potential new opportunities before your competition can—almost as if you get to become part of the customer's planning process. I don't believe I need to say anything more about the advantage you have when you initiate an opportunity rather than react to one.

- Measure results that are crucial to developing effective job aids for stimulating interest with prospective buyers, especially Value Propositions and Reference Stories.

In this chapter, you'll find principles, exercises, and job aids that help you to measure and leverage the customer's success. Those Solution Selling job aids are

Success Criteria

Reference Stories

The following example shows what the Success Criteria metrics might look like for a customer one year after implementation. This is not to say that you have to wait a full year to be able create new job aids for stimulating interest—you don't. Some of the criteria will provide positive metrics sooner than others will.

In this example, the criterion "number of customer service reps" immediately shows positive results, while "credit write-offs per quarter" doesn't. It may be appropriate to create progress-to-date Value Propositions and Reference Stories around specific elements rather than for all the Success Criteria.

Success Criteria Example

Success Criteria	Baseline	Q1	Q2	Q3	Q4
Average # of new accounts per rep per quarter (1)	2.5	2.75	3	3	3.25
Web site orders placed per customer (1)	0%	5%	7%	10%	16%
Number of referrals per quarter (1)	7.5	8	10	13	12
Credit write-offs per quarter (2)	$200K	$200K	$150K	$100K	$100K
Number of customer service reps (2)	18	17	16	15	14
Sources of data: (1) VP Sales (2) VP Finance					

Continuing the Value Cycle

Measuring the Success Criteria provides results. For every customer individual who benefits from the implementation of your offering, a Reference Story and a Value Proposition can be created that focus on how this particular situation was addressed. This is where the value cycle continues. The measurement of the criteria allows the results to be extrapolated and projected onto prospective buyers. This allows you to lead with value when starting new opportunities.

For example, you might specifically look at a set of metrics as they relate to the Vice President of Finance. Using these figures, you could create a new Reference Story or a new Value Proposition

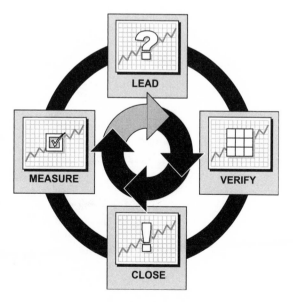

to stimulate interest and create new opportunities by targeting financial officers in other prospect organizations.

Success Criteria	Baseline	Q1	Q2	Q3	Q4
Credit write-offs per quarter (2)	$200K	$200K	$150K	$100K	$100K

Using this information, you can create a new Reference Story that describes how your organization helped a Vice President of Finance address a business issue of not meeting profit targets because the company's credit write-offs were excessive.

New Reference Story Example

Situation:	VP Finance, manufacturing industry
Critical business issue:	Not meeting profit targets
One reason:	Increasing amount of bad debt write-offs
Capabilities:	He said his company needed a way . . .
[*when*]:	Prior to accepting an online order,
[*who*]:	for his Web site
[*what*]:	to alert the customer to the outstanding credit issue and connect the customer to the accounting department automatically
We provided:	him with those capabilities.
Result:	Within one year his overall bad debt write-offs had been reduced by 50% ($250K), which contributed greatly to his meeting overall profit targets.

EXERCISE: MEASURING YOUR SUCCESS CRITERIA
Activities

- Measure the Success Criteria that you established in Chapter 11 ("Exercise: Determining Your Success Criteria").

- Use the same worksheet provided for that exercise.

- Compare the quarterly metrics to the established baseline to determine which criteria are tracking well and which ones are tracking poorly.

Notes

- This exercise will take place over months, quarters, and longer periods. Stay committed to the measurement and leverage your success to build new job aids for stimulating interest, as discussed in Chapter 4.

- New worksheets and templates can be found in Appendix B, "Solution Selling Job Aid Templates."

Summary

The benefits of measuring Success Criteria are as valuable to you as they are to the customer. Ensuring the customer's success ensures your own.

PART FIVE

MANAGING YOUR OPPORTUNITIES

CHAPTER 14

HOW TO MANAGE YOUR OPPORTUNITIES

Let's play the word association game. What is the first image that comes to mind when I mention the phrase "traditional sales manager"? If you're like many sales professionals, the traditional picture that develops is that of an overbearing boss who frequently calls his or her salespeople into the office to repeatedly ask questions such as, "How's the opportunity going?" "When is it going to close?" and "Are you going to make quota?"

This "micro-managing" stereotype has been the classic management style used by sales managers for decades. Don't misunderstand—I think that gathering important information from salespeople is a critical role for sales managers. After all, they have a boss, too. However, sales managers can get the information they need more efficiently and effectively by enabling the salespeople to have more control over the management of their opportunities. This is a different style of management. I call it "macro-managing."

When salespeople have a good sales process and are armed with effective job aids, they will clearly see the role of managing the sales process as one in which they should and want to participate.

There are multiple steps, exercises, and management job aids comprising the Solution Selling sales management methodology. In this chapter, I have included a select group that will help you manage your pipeline and opportunities.

In this chapter, you'll be introduced to

- *Solution Selling Pipeline Milestones* A checklist of Solution Selling sales activities that comprises individual milestones in the sales process. It helps you to recognize which milestone you have passed and to identify your next steps.

- *Pipeline Milestone Worksheet* A worksheet that provides a collective view of your opportunities and the actual completion dates for each of the sales activities (found in the Solution Selling Pipeline Milestones). It helps you to identify opportunities that are potentially stalled and recognize potential skill challenges.

- *Pipeline Analysis Worksheet* A worksheet that assists you in determining the potential revenue yield of your current and future pipeline. It helps you to determine at any time of the year your likelihood of attaining your sales goals.

In the figures that follow, you will see the Solution Selling Pipeline Milestones and a view of how the milestones would be found within the Solution Selling process flow model first introduced in Chapter 2. The milestones and sales activities provide a common language for accurately communicating progress within an opportunity.

Solution Selling Pipeline Milestones

Milestone	Milestone description	Sales activities
T	**Territory**	☐ Opportunity identified in territory
S	**Qualified Suspect**	☐ Meets marketing criteria ☐ Potential sponsor identified ☐ Initial contact established (verifiable)
D	**Qualified Sponsor**	☐ Pain admitted by sponsor ☐ Sponsor has a valued buying vision ☐ Sponsor agreed to explore ☐ Access to power negotiated ☐ Agreed to above in Sponsor Letter
C	**Qualified Power Sponsor**	☐ Access to power sponsor ☐ Pain admitted by power sponsor ☐ Power sponsor has a valued buying vision ☐ Power sponsor agreed to explore ☐ Evaluation Plan proposed ☐ Evaluation Plan agreed upon
		☐ Evaluation Plan underway ☐ Pre-proposal review conducted ☐ Asked for the business ☐ Proposal issued, decision due ☐ Verbal approval received
B	**Decision Due**	☐ Contract negotiation in progress
A	**Pending Sale**	☐ Signed documents
W	**Win**	☐ Update prospect database

Solution Selling Process Flow Model with Pipeline Milestone

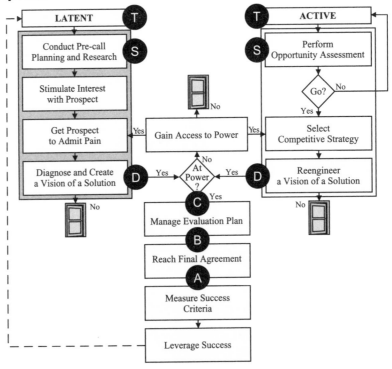

Pipeline Milestone Worksheet

Use the Pipeline Milestone Worksheet to record each opportunitys name; the opportunity's origin (latent or active); an estimated potential sale amount (in thousands of dollars), and the dates of completion for each activity.

Pipeline Milestone Worksheet

← Days in Code		Opportunity Name →	1	2	3	4	5	6	7	8	9	10	
													Latent or active opportunity (L or A)
													Potential sale amount ($K)
—	T												Opportunity identified in territory
													Meets marketing criteria
													Potential sponsor identified
	S												Initial contact established (verifiable)
													Pain admitted by sponsor
													Sponsor has a valued buying vision
													Sponsor agreed to explore
													Access to power negotiated
	D												Agreed to above in Sponsor Letter
													Access to power sponsor
													Pain admitted by power sponsor
—													Power sponsor has a valued buying vision
													Power sponsor agreed to explore
													Evaluation Plan proposed
	C												Evaluation Plan agreed upon
													Evaluation Plan underway
													Pre-proposal review conducted
—													Asked for the business
													Proposal issued, decision due*
	B												Verbal approval received
—	A												Contract negotiation in process
—	W												Signed documents
—													Update prospect database

*Premature delivery of a proposal may *not* be a sign of progress.

Once the opportunity information has been recorded, you can compare the time you typically spend at a particular milestone against the actual time spent. This can help to identify potential stalls in your opportunities. You can determine the typical time in code by referring to the table that follows.

Typical Time in Code Table

The following table provides an estimate of the typical number of days spent accomplishing the sales activities within each milestone. When my clients customize the list of sales activities for their organization, I always encourage them to reevaluate the time frames indicated here. However, these time frames are based on years of experience executing the steps of Solution Selling and provide a good starting point.

Milestone	Sell Cycle Length in Months					
	3 months	4 months	6 months	8 months	9 months	12 months
S	9	15	15	15	15	15
D	18	24	30	30	35	40
C	30	42	90	150	170	250
B	18	24	30	30	35	40
A	11	11	11	11	11	11
W	4	4	4	4	4	4

EXERCISE: FILL OUT THE PIPELINE MILESTONE WORKSHEET, PART I

Activities

- Determine your typical sell cycle length in months.

- Record the number of days spent accomplishing the sales activities that lead to each milestone, as indicated in the Typical Time in Code Table.

- Record those figures in the spaces provided in the column headed "Days in Code," found on the Pipeline Milestone Worksheet.

- Enter the information for each opportunity you are working on in one of the columns provided (opportunity name, latent or active, potential sale amount, and a date for each sales activity accomplished) on the Pipeline Milestone Worksheet.

- Analyze each opportunity to determine if any of them are stalled. Do this by looking at the last date recorded in relation to the number of days that should be spent reaching the given milestone. Any opportunities that appear to be lagging beyond the expected date by several days or more may require exceptional attention. Circle the last date for the opportunities that may be stalled.

Note: This exercise is an iterative one that should be performed periodically to ensure that each opportunity is progressing through the pipeline.

EXERCISE: FILL OUT THE PIPELINE MILESTONE WORKSHEET, PART II

Activities

- Address each stalled opportunity:
  - Ensure that all sales activities have been completed. If any have been skipped, this may be causing the stall. Go back and attempt to accomplish the activity.
  - Analyze the actions taken and the quality of information gathered at each milestone in order to identify a reason why the opportunity may have stalled.
  - Use the Potential Selling Difficulties Table that follows to help identify the likely reason. For any difficulty identified as a reason for the stall, go back and attempt to accomplish the step again, seeking to improve on the action previously taken or the quality of the information gathered.

Milestone Stall	Potential Selling Difficulties
From S to D	■ Getting the sponsor to admit a high-priority *pain* ■ Effectively creating or reengineering a buying *vision* ■ Effectively positioning the *value* of addressing the buying vision ■ Determining who *power* is and/or gaining access to them
From D to C	■ Validating *power's* ability to buy ■ Getting the *power* sponsor to admit a high-priority *pain* ■ Effectively creating or reengineering a buying *vision* ■ Effectively positioning the *value* of addressing the buying vision ■ Getting power sponsor "buy-in" to the Evaluation Plan (*control*)
From C to B	■ Delivered a proposal prematurely (loss of *control*) ■ Positioned *value* justification that is not compelling ■ Created poor alignment with buyer (e.g., showed proof too early)
From B to A	■ Difficulty negotiating

Selling Skill or Opportunity Challenge?

See if the "potential selling difficulty" identified for one opportunity exists across multiple opportunities. If not, the difficulty may be opportunity-related and require short-term attention as suggested by the previous recommendations. If a pattern is identified, however, a challenge with a particular selling skill may exist and attention may be required.

If the selling skill is related to

- *Pain* Revisit the content and exercises found in Chapters 3 through 5.

- *Power* Revisit the content and exercises found in Chapters 9 and 10.

- *Vision* Revisit the content and exercises found in Chapters 6 through 8.

- *Value* Revisit the content and exercises found in Chapters 6 and 11.

- *Control* Revisit the content and exercises found in Chapters 10 through 12.

You have analyzed your opportunities to ensure that they are properly coded with the correct milestone, and you have addressed ones that are stalled. Now you are in a much better position to determine the potential revenue yield of your current and future pipeline.

Yield

Yield is an estimate of the revenue value in a pipeline that is expected to be realized. It is calculated by multiplying the revenue associated with each milestone by the milestone's win rate percentage, sometimes called the yield percentage.

Just as I encourage clients to customize the sales activities of the pipeline milestones for their organization, I encourage them to apply their own win rates to their defined milestones. The win rates of the Solution Selling Pipeline Milestones (S = 10 percent, D = 25 percent, C = 50 percent, B = 75 percent, A = 90 percent, W = 100 percent) are based on years of experience in executing the steps and measuring the results. They provide a good starting point.

The Pipeline Analysis Worksheet takes into consideration these win rates, the current pipeline, year-to-date attainment, and other factors to help answer the question, "Will I make my goal or quota?"

Pipeline Analysis Worksheet

A	Quota:					
B	Average sell time:					
C	Average size of opportunities ($)					
D	Current month:					
E	Year-to-date attainment not reflected in Ws ($):					
F	Milestone Code	Revenue	×	Win Odds		Yield
	S	$	×	10%	=	$
	D	$	×	25%	=	$
	C	$	×	50%	=	$
	B	$	×	75%	=	$
	A	$	×	90%	=	$
	W	$	×	100%	=	$
				Total yield in pipeline:		$
G	Revenue underway (E + F):					$
H	Shortfall to go (A − G):					$
I	Likely additional yield (F ÷ B × number of months left to sell):					$
J	Remaining shortfall to go (H − I):					$
K	New Ss required (J ÷ C × 10):					

EXERCISE: ANALYZE YOUR PIPELINE

Activities

- Fill out the Pipeline Analysis Worksheet to determine if you will achieve your goal or quota for the year or if there is a gap.

- Use information from the filled-out Pipeline Milestone Worksheet to help with this exercise (i.e., potential sale amount, milestone code, and so on).

- Determine what actions you can take to improve your chances of closing the gap if one does exist. See the suggestions provided in the next section.

Notes:

- You may want to calculate C (average size of opportunities in $) by estimating your average size of opportunities based on your own experience or, if a total dollar volume is known, by dividing that number by the number of opportunities you have in the pipeline.

- If you have an actual corporate pipeline report with information that supports this exercise, be sure to use it.

- Using yield calculations to determine if you will make your quota becomes more effective when a large number of opportunities are found in the pipeline.

What If a Gap Does Exist?

If a gap does exist, there are several actions that you might take. Some of these actions will be more effective than others, based on the time of year of the analysis.

If a gap exists:

- *Increase your win odds* Using the Opportunity Assessment Worksheet can help you put opportunities in your pipeline that are more qualified and avoid the ones that are not.

- *Shorten your sell cycle* Using Evaluation Plans can help you control the buying process and put buyers in a position to make a purchasing and implementation decision more quickly.

- *Increase the size of your opportunities* Using the Pain Chain can show a buying organization the impact across the organization. This can enable you to cross-sell or up-sell other products and services.

- *Find more S opportunities* Using the stimulating interest job aids during prospecting will help create interest and put more opportunities into the pipeline

Summary

When you have a good sales process and are armed with effective job aids, you see the role of managing your sales process as one in which you should participate. Solution Selling provides a framework for enabling you to have more control over the management of your opportunities.

AFTERWORD

Now that you have read and applied the Solution Selling concepts to specific situations, it is important that you continue to use and refine what you have learned. Let me encourage you to continue to use *The Solution Selling Fieldbook*, the CD-ROM, and the Solution Selling Software as resources to help you attain your highest professional goals.

As you continue to apply the Solution Selling methodology to your own sales situations, take comfort in knowing that you are not alone. More than 500,000 people use Solution Selling every day. I encourage you to join our growing community of Solution Selling devotees by participating in our free online Sales Community on the Web, which can be found at http://www.solutionselling.com.

If you'd like more information about how to implement Solution Selling in your own organization, please contact us at:

Sales Performance International

6230 Fairview Road, Suite 200

Charlotte, NC 28210 USA

Phone: (704) 364-9298

Fax: (704) 364-8114

E-mail: info@spisales.com

Web: http://www.spisales.com

We intend to update and refine this book in future editions. To that end, we'd be delighted to receive your comments and suggestions for improvement. Just drop us an e-mail message at Fieldbook@spisales.com.

Finally, I wish you courage in your efforts to implement Solution Selling and optimism in realizing the freedom that comes from success.

Good luck and good selling!

SOLUTION SELLING REFERENCE SECTION

HOW TO USE THE CD-ROM

In the back of this fieldbook, you'll find a CD-ROM that contains

- Solution Selling job aid templates in Microsoft Word format

- Internet links to helpful Solution Selling resources

- Installation files for a fully functional trial copy of the single-user version of the Solution Selling Software application

Hardware and Software Requirements

To use the CD-ROM included with this fieldbook, you will need

- An IBM-compatible personal computer (PC) running the Microsoft Windows operating system—either the Windows XP (recommended) or Windows 2000 version

- A drive capable of reading a CD-ROM formatted disk

To use the Solution Selling job aid templates, you will also need an installed copy of Microsoft Word, version 2000 or higher recommended, or a word processing application that can read Microsoft Word formatted files.

To use the Internet links, you will also need to establish an Internet connection, either dial-up or broadband (DSL or cable). A broadband connection is highly recommended. You will also need an Internet browser application, such as Microsoft Internet Explorer version 6.0 or higher or Mozilla Firefox version 1.0 or higher.

To use the trial copy of the Solution Selling Software application, you will also need

- The authority (power user or administrator at a minimum) to install new software on your PC

- A minimum screen resolution of 1,024 × 768

- The ability to establish a broadband Internet connection (DSL or cable)

Using the Solution Selling Job Aid Templates

Templates for all the job aids contained in this fieldbook have been provided in Microsoft Word format. To install them for use on your PC, insert the CD-ROM into your computer. After a few seconds, a menu of options should appear on your screen. Select the "Solution Selling Job Aids" button on the menu.

You will see a Windows directory of all the templates on the CD-ROM. You can select these files, copy them to your system, or open them directly from the CD-ROM. Just remember that you can't save any edited files on your CD-ROM—you have to save them on your PC's storage disks.

The CD-ROM includes all the following Solution Selling job aid templates:

- Key Players List

- Account Profile

- Pain Chain

- Business Development Prompter
- Business Development Letter
- Reference Story
- Value Proposition
- Strategic Alignment Prompter
- Opportunity Assessment Worksheet
- Competitive Strategy Selector
- 9 Block Vision Processing Model—Vision Creation
- 9 Block Vision Processing Model—Vision Reengineering
- Pain Sheet
- RFP Initial Response Letter
- RFP Executive Summary
- Sponsor Letter (or e-mail) for Vision Creation
- Sponsor Letter (or e-mail) for Vision Reengineering
- Power Sponsor Letter (or e-mail)
- Evaluation Plan
- Go/No-Go Step Completion Letter
- Value Justification Model
- Success Criteria
- Negotiating Worksheet
- Anxiety Creation
- Transition Issues and Capabilities Worksheet
- Implementation Plan Letter (or e-mail)
- Implementation (Transition) Plan
- Solution Selling Pipeline Milestones
- Pipeline Milestone Worksheet (including Time-in-Code Table)
- Pipeline Analysis Worksheet

For a description of how to use each of these templates, see the appropriate section in Appendix B, "Solution Selling Job Aid Templates."

Accessing the Internet Links

We've provided some helpful Internet links to further your understanding of Solution Selling and to connect you with additional resources that may be helpful. To use these links, insert the CD-ROM into your computer. After a few seconds, a menu of options should appear on your screen. Select the "Internet Links" button on the menu.

You will see a Windows directory of HTML files. By double-clicking your cursor on any of these files, you will launch your Internet browser application. If you have established an Internet connection successfully, you will then be connected to an Internet Web page.

The CD-ROM includes the following Internet links for your use:

- The Sales Performance International Web site, where you'll have access to more information about Solution Selling training and implementation resources.

- The Solution Selling Online e-Learning program, where you can receive additional online training in Solution Selling at a nominal fee.

- The "Best Practices" section of the SPI web site, where you'll find free white papers and recorded Web seminars on sales best practices. You can also register to receive a free electronic newsletter on Solution Selling.

- The SPI Sales Community Web site, where you'll find the latest free information about the best use of Solution Selling in the field.

- The Solution Selling Software Web site, where you can download the latest version and learn more about application software support available for the Solution Selling methodology.

Once you have connected to any of these Web sites, be sure to save them to your "Favorites" list or bookmark them for future reference, as your Internet browser application requires.

Installing the Solution Selling Software

We've provided a fully functional trial copy of the single-user version of the Solution Selling Software application on the CD-ROM. This integrated application supports all of the Solution Selling job aids and tools in an easy-to-use automated interface.

Once installed, this application will run on your PC for 21 days. If you like the application, you can purchase a one-year renewable license for just $195. (You can also purchase a licensed version of the application by going to http://www.spitools.com and completing the registration process.)

To install the trial Solution Selling Software application, insert the **CD-ROM** into your computer. After a few seconds, a menu of options should appear on your screen. Select the "Solution Selling Software" button on the menu.

Your Internet browser application will open the download menu for the Solution Selling Software. Select the "Download Trial Version" button for Solution Selling Software: Professional, and then follow the prompts as they appear.

While the Microsoft Word templates provided on the CD-ROM are certainly useful, the Solution Selling Software application is much easier to use. In addition, this application contains a number of features that make the use of the Solution Selling methodology more practical and, frankly, more fun.

The software contains automated support for

- All job aids established within the Solution Selling methodology, including
  - Account Profile
  - Pipeline Milestones
  - Organizational Chart
  - Pain Chain
  - Business Development Prompter
  - Reference Story
  - Call Debrief

- ○ Value Proposition
- ○ Pain Sheets
- ○ Anxiety Creation
- ○ Opportunity Assessment
- ○ Evaluation Plan
- ○ Transition Issues
- ○ Value Justification
- ○ Success Criteria
- ○ Negotiating Worksheet
- ○ Implementation Plan
- ○ Prospect Qualification Worksheet
- ○ Pipeline Milestone Worksheet
- ○ Pipeline Analysis Worksheet
- ○ A comprehensive list of Solution Selling letter/e-mail templates
- ○ Integrated coaching on Solution Selling methods and techniques

- Data import and export capabilities, allowing sharing of sales opportunities and job aids with other members of your sales team

- Printing, e-mailing, and saving of reports in several formats, including Microsoft Word (.doc), Adobe Acrobat (.pdf), Rich Text Format (.rtf), and Microsoft PowerPoint (.ppt)

Technical and user support for Solution Selling Software is readily available through the Web at http://www.spitools.com, backed by a multichannel contact center.

Getting Started with Solution Selling Software

If you've read this book, or if you've attended a Solution Selling workshop, you'll find the use of Solution Selling Software to be intuitive. But here are a few tips to get you started:

- If you need help, click on the Help icon in the upper right corner of the screen—the one that looks like a balloon with a question mark (?) in it.

- Open Help and review the "Getting Started" materials for an overview of the application.

- To begin analysis of an opportunity,
  1. Click on "Portfolio Manager."
  2. Click on "Create" under "Account" and enter the account name of the prospect.
  3. Click on "Create" under "Opportunity" and enter what you expect to sell.
  4. Use the various Solution Selling job aids by clicking on their names in the left column.

- Remember to save your work before closing the application.

SOLUTION SELLING JOB AID TEMPLATES

Solution Selling Job Aid Templates

- Key Players List
- Account Profile
- Pain Chain
- Business Development Prompter
- Business Development Letter
- Reference Story
- Value Proposition
- Strategic Alignment Prompter
- Opportunity Assessment Worksheet
- Competitive Strategy Selector
- 9 Block Vision Processing Model—Vision Creation

- 9 Block Vision Processing Model—Vision Reengineering
- Pain Sheet
- RFP Initial Response Letter
- RFP Executive Summary
- Sponsor Letter (or e-mail) for Vision Creation
- Sponsor Letter (or e-mail) for Vision Reengineering
- Power Sponsor Letter (or e-mail)
- Evaluation Plan
- Go/No-Go Step Completion Letter
- Value Justification Model
- Success Criteria
- Negotiating Worksheet

Additional Solution Selling Job Aids, Examples, and Templates

- Anxiety Creation
- Transition Issues and Capabilities Worksheet
- Implementation Plan Letter (or e-mail)
- Implementation (Transition) Plan

Job Aids for Managing Your Opportunities

- Solution Selling Pipeline Milestones
- Pipeline Milestone Worksheet (including Time in Code Table)
- Pipeline Analysis Worksheet

Key Players List

Overview

The Key Players List is a listing by industry of important job titles along with the critical business issues (pains) that people with that job title (key players) are likely to face.

Where/How Used

The Key Players List helps you identify pains to probe for when marketing to, calling on, or meeting with a particular buyer based on that buyer's job title and role. This is especially helpful when calling on a buyer or within an industry where you have less experience or that you are unfamiliar with.

The Key Players List can be used to initiate sales opportunities by identifying latent pains that buyers have not yet recognized. It also can be used to identify the underlying pain that has driven a buyer to commit to action in an active sell cycle.

What You Should Achieve

By using the Key Players List, you should be able to identify key players and their potential pains more quickly. This list can also help you develop your situational knowledge and experience in a given industry.

Input Required

To create a Key Players List, you must research the key players, their pains, and their job titles within your target industries.

Note: The ideal situation is to have a database of Key Players Lists for the industries and job titles you typically encounter. These lists should be updated periodically to reflect new information resulting from industry trends and customer interactions.

Key Players List Template

Industry:	
Job Title	**Pains**
	• _____ • _____ • _____ • _____ • _____ • _____ • _____
	• _____ • _____ • _____ • _____ • _____ • _____ • _____
	• _____ • _____ • _____ • _____ • _____ • _____ • _____
	• _____ • _____ • _____ • _____ • _____ • _____ • _____
	• _____ • _____ • _____ • _____ • _____ • _____ • _____

Account Profile

Overview

A brief overview of a target company that describes particular elements of the organization. The profile highlights the challenges the organization is facing.

Where/How Used

The Account Profile serves as an ideal "quick information" resource for you to gain insight about an account with which you are about to make contact. The profile should include

- Overview of the company
- Description of its offerings
- Analysis of its markets
- Summary of its financial status
- Description of its competition
- Executive biographies
- Descriptions of potential pains
- Potential capabilities needed

What You Should Achieve

The Account Profile should help you or your team to strategize how to move forward with a potential opportunity by identifying specific pains that the organization is likely to be facing. Additionally, identification of key players within the organization and their pains will start to formulate a picture of how the individuals' pains are connected in a cause-and-effect relationship.

Input Required

Knowledge of the prospect's organization, the key players, and the pains they are likely to be facing—a Key Players List for the industry will be useful.

Note: Account Profiles can be supplemented by corporate information such as account plans or customer relationship management data. There are also many third-party organizations that can serve as a resource for researching and providing the latest information on accounts. A complete Account Profile represents the minimum amount of information that should be known before engaging with an opportunity.

Account Profile Template

Overview of the company

Description of its offerings

Analysis of its markets

Summary of its financial status

Description of its competition

Executive biographies, including descriptions of potential pains

Potential capabilities needed

Pain Chain

Overview
The Pain Chain is a graphical depiction of the cause-and-effect relationship of critical business issues (pains) inside an organization. It includes job title, pain, and the reasons for that pain.

Where/How Used
The Pain Chain is used in pre-call planning and research to better understand potential interdependencies in an opportunity.

In addition, after interviewing individuals to validate your assumptions, you can recraft your initial Pain Chain to reflect your new findings. Sharing this level of information with buyers during the sell cycle can help establish further credibility.

What You Should Achieve
A completed Pain Chain demonstrates to the buyer an insightful understanding of his or her business.

Input Required
To create a Pain Chain, you must understand the pains of key players in the organization and the reasons for their pains

Pain Chain Template

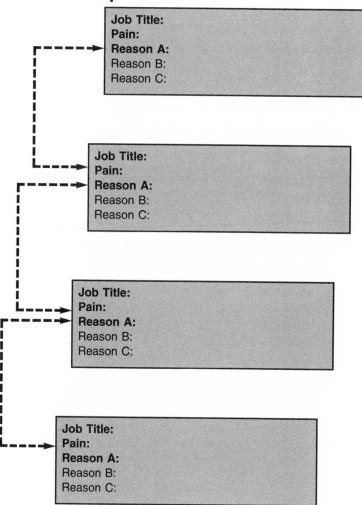

Business Development Prompter

Overview
A Business Development Prompter is a very brief, targeted script used to increase the success rate of stimulating interest.

Where/How Used
A Business Development Prompter is usually used to initiate contact over the telephone. The objective is to stimulate interest in order to motivate the prospect to want to learn about your products and services. The prompter can be modified for various approaches, but most versions should include these elements:

- Your name
- Your organization
- The targeted industry
- Number of years of experience within that industry
- A description of a pain experienced by others with a job title or role similar to that of the prospect and within the same or a similar industry as that of the prospect
- A concise framework that allows the message to be delivered in under 30 seconds

What You Should Achieve
The purpose of using the Business Development Prompter is to have the prospect become curious enough to want to set up a future appointment or to ask to continue listening on the phone to learn how a peer has already solved a similar problem that she or he might have or can relate to.

Input Required
To build the Business Development Prompter, you will need knowledge of how you or your organization has helped other

buyers (by title) solve pains within the targeted industry. Prior customer successes and Key Players Lists can be useful as input.

Note: The key elements of a Business Development Prompter for new prospects can also be modified to create variations of the prompter that emphasize a menu of pains approach, a customer referral approach, and so on. The key elements of a Business Development Prompter can also be used in written correspondence. See the discussion of Business Development Letters or e-mails that follows.

Business Development Prompter Templates

New Opportunity Option

This is _____ [*your name*] with _____
[*your organization*]. You and I haven't spoken before, but our company has been working with _____ [*target industry*] for the last _____ [*#*] years. One of the chief concerns we are hearing [*lately*] from other _____ [*job title*] is their frustration/difficulty with _____ [*job title's likely critical issue/pain*].

We have been able to help our customers address this issue. Would you like to know how?

Menu of Pains Option

This is _____ [*your name*] with _____
[*your organization*]. You and I haven't spoken before, but our company has been working with _____ [*target industry*] for the last _____ [*#*] years. The top three issues/concerns we are hearing (lately) from other _____ [*job title*] are:
(1) _____,
(2) _____, and
(3) _____
      [*job title's top three likely critical business issues/pains*].

We have helped companies like _____, _____, and _____ [*three reference organizations*] address some of these issues. Would you be curious in learning how?

Customer Referral Option

This is _____ [*your name*] with _____
[*your organization*]. You and I haven't spoken before, but
_____, _____ at
_____ [*reference person's name, title, and organization*], suggested that I give you a call.
We were able to help (her/him) address (his/her) frustration/difficulty with
_____
      [*reference person's critical business issue/pain*].
Would you be interested to know how?

Business Development Letter

Overview
The Business Development Letter is similar to the Business Development Prompter. It is a proactive letter or e-mail sent to stimulate interest and move a prospect from latent pain to admitted pain.

Where/How Used
The Business Development Letter is used to cold-mail prospects. The objective is to stimulate interest in order to motivate the prospect to want to learn about your products and services.

What You Should Achieve
The Business Development Letter should move the prospect from not looking to looking and should stimulate enough interest to have the prospect contact you or your organization for additional information. As part of your overall business development strategy, you may choose to send the Business Development Letter (e-mail) to a prospect and then follow it up with a call relating elements of the Business Development Prompter.

Input Required
To create a Business Development Letter, you must have references and success stories of closed opportunities that information can be extracted from. The letter should contain the following elements:

- A benefit statement about your organization's core competency

- A statement highlighting your organization's experience in the targeted industry

- A description of multiple high-probability pains that the prospect may have

- Approved customer names to be used as references

Business Development Letter Template

Dear _____ [*prospect*],

Our company is in the business of helping our customers _____
_____
[*describe positioning statement using a "we help" theme*].

We have been working with _____ [*industry*] companies for ___ [*#*] years.
Our clients include [*three reference customer organizations*]:

_____ ,

_____ , and

_____ .

Some of the chief concerns we hear from them are [*top three potential pains*]:

_____ ,

_____ , and

_____ .

We have been able to help our customers successfully deal with these
and other issues. I would like an opportunity to share some examples with
you. If you are interested in learning how we have helped other
_____ [*job title*] solve some very challenging issues,
please call me at _____ [*phone number*] and I will provide
you with more information.

Sincerely, _____

Reference Story

Overview
The Reference Story is a job aid that provides you with a conversational prompter that helps you to stimulate interest, build credibility with a prospect, and get the prospect to admit pain. It gives you an opportunity to share a situationally specific story of how the prospect's peers have been helped by implementing capabilities provided by your organization.

Where/How Used
The Reference Story is used as a prompter, not a script. It is typically used as part of the "stimulating interest" step of the Solution Selling process, but it can be used effectively to assist in building credibility, getting pain admitted, and demonstrating proof at multiple stages in a sell cycle.

What You Should Achieve
When a Reference Story is used successfully,

- The prospect will feel comfortable enough to admit the pain.

- The prospect may divulge that she or he already has a vision of a solution.

- Enough credibility will be established that you will have earned the right to continue further conversation with the prospect.

Input Required
To create a Reference Story, you must have specific examples from previous successful opportunities and know the measurable results that were achieved.

Note: The ideal situation is to have a database of Reference Stories cataloged by the industries and job titles you are targeting. Additional Reference Stories should be added to the database as customers recognize results.

Reference Story Template

Situation:	_____
Pain:	_____
	_____
Reason(s):	_____
	_____
Capabilities: _When, who, what:_	"He/she/they said they needed a way to . . ."
	_____
	_____
	_____
We provided:	"We provided him/her/them with those capabilities."
Result:	_____
	_____

Value Proposition

Overview

A Value Proposition is a statement that *projects* the quantified value that a prospect should achieve through the use of your organization's capabilities. It is intended to stimulate interest and serve as the catalyst to begin an evaluation of your capabilities.

Where/How Used

Value Propositions can be used at any time or any place with a prospective buyer. They are most commonly used when you want to stimulate interest. After interest is stimulated, the Value Proposition serves as the basis point to work from with the prospect. After interest has been generated, the logical steps that follow should be to verify or revise the projections.

What You Should Achieve

The Value Proposition should help you stimulate a prospective buyer's interest and build credibility for you and your organization.

Input Required

To create a Value Proposition, you must have specific knowledge of the results and value already achieved by an existing customer. You will also need to know specific baseline information about the prospect you are targeting. Results found in customer Reference Stories provide a great source of data from which to extrapolate. Third-party sources such as OneSource provide good baseline metrics on the prospective buyer's business.

Value Proposition Template

We believe that _____ [*prospect organization's name*]

should be able to _____

[*describe pain being addressed or area being improved*]

by _____ [*how much in % and/or $*]

through the ability to _____

[*describe primary benefit*]

as a result of _____

[*describe primary capability or enabler of offering/s*]

for an approximate investment of _____

[*prospect's relative investment $*].

Value proposition assumptions:
-
-
-

 Strategic Alignment Prompter

Overview
The Strategic Alignment Prompter is a seven-step guide that helps you align your selling activities with the buying process, starting with a first call or initial conversation.

Where/How Used
The Strategic Alignment Prompter provides a framework that can be used to execute the activities of a first face-to-face meet-

ing or first phone call. It should help you to identify when and how to

1. Establish rapport.

2. State the objective of the call and provide information that
   - Positions your organization.
   - Provides facts that allow the prospect to draw positive conclusions about you, your organization, and your offerings.
   - Shares a relevant Reference Story.

3. Lead the prospect to admit pain.

4. Develop the customer's needs.

5. Gain agreement to move forward.

6. Determine the prospect's ability to buy.

7. Either negotiate for access to power or qualify the buying and evaluation criteria with power.

What You Should Achieve

Successful alignment should initially provide you with an opportunity to demonstrate to a prospect that you are sincere and competent, thereby earning the right to continue exploring the prospect's situation. Continued alignment through the steps of the Strategic Alignment Prompter should result in the prospect's admitting pain and developing a vision of a solution that will resolve the pain, ending with a sense of mutual commitment between the salesperson and the prospect concerning the next steps.

Input Required

The Strategic Alignment Prompter, Steps 1 to 3, requires a call objective, a company positioning statement, company facts, and a Reference Story.

Strategic Alignment Prompter

Step 1: Establish Rapport

☐ **Let the prospect set the tone of the meeting**

"I appreciate the opportunity to meet with you."
Read the need for "small talk" or "business talk."

Step 2: Introduce Call

☐ **State the call objective**

"What I would like to do today (*or* during the next _____ minutes) is to
- Introduce you to _____ [*your company name*] and
- Tell you about another _____ [*job title*] in the
  _____ industry [*specific industry*] we have worked with.
- I would then like to learn about you and your situation.
- Then the two of us will be able to make a mutual decision as to whether or not we should proceed any further."

☐ **Share a positioning statement (use "we help" theme)**

"[*Your company name*] is in the business of helping organizations in the
_____ industry [*specific industry*] _____
_____
_____."

☐ **Provide a company and personal introduction**

Conclusions		Facts
	⇔	
	⇔	
	⇔	

☐ **Share a relevant reference story or progress-to-date anecdote**

"A particular situation you might be interested in is another _____ [*organization type*]. Its _____ [*job title*] was having difficulty with _____ [*pain*]. The reasons for his/her difficulty were _____. What he/she said was needed was a way to _____. We provided him/her with those capabilities. And the result was _____."

☐ **Make the transition to getting pain admitted**

"But enough about [*how we helped another organization*]. Tell me about you and your situation."

Step 3: Get Pain Admitted

If pain has not been admitted:
- But the buyer is talking freely → ask situation questions.
- And the buyer is not talking freely → ask pain or menu of pain questions.

Once pain is admitted, prioritize it.

Strategic Alignment Prompter (continued)

Step 4: Develop Needs: Customer Buying Vision

☐ **Use the 9 Block Vision Processing Model**

    ☐ Diagnose and create a vision of a company-biased solution *or*
    ☐ Reengineer a vision with company differentiators

☐ **Confirm buying vision and bridge to "Agreement to Move Forward" step**

"So, if you had the ability to [*restate capabilities*], could you [*restate goal*]?" [*Get buyer's agreement.*]

Step 5: Gain Agreement to Move Forward

<u>Option 1:</u>
"[*Buyer's name*], I am reasonably sure that we can provide you with those capabilities. I want to check some things with my resources. If they confirm what we just discussed, will you further evaluate [*company*]?" [*Get buyer's agreement.*]

<u>Option 2:</u>
"[*Buyer's name*], I'm confident that we can provide you with those capabilities, and I would like the opportunity to prove it to you. Would you give me that opportunity?" [*Get buyer's agreement.*]

If during the process, the buyer volunteered access to power, schedule the meeting and end the call. If the buyer did not volunteer access to power, go to Step 6

Step 6: Determine Ability to Buy

"Let's say you become convinced that it really is possible to [*repeat buying vision*] and you want to go forward. What do you do then? Who else is involved?"

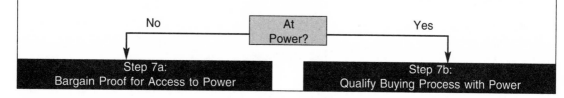

No	At Power?	Yes
Step 7a: Bargain Proof for Access to Power		**Step 7b:** Qualify Buying Process with Power

Strategic Alignment Prompter (continued)

Step 7a: Bargain Proof for Access to Power	Step 7b: Qualify Buying Process with Power
❑ Negotiate for access to power	❑ Ask open questions, set up ground rules for proposal
"Could we get on his/her calendar?" [*If denied, strike a bargain.*]	"How would you like to evaluate us?" [*Write down each request as you repeat it. Do not agree or disagree.*]
❑ Strike a bargain (for access to power)	If we get to a point where we might want to do business, will there be a . . . [*legal review? technical review? administrative approval?*]
"It may be premature at this point, but let me suggest this. I'm not yet sure of the best way for us to prove these capabilities to you. I first want to consult with my resources.	Will you want a proposal from me? [*Get buyer's agreement.*] As part of that proposal, will you also want a value analysis?"
Which ever method we end up using [*to prove these capabilities*], it will take some of my company's resources. I'm willing to make that commitment today.	❑ State "no new information" and pre-proposal review themes
If through that effort we succeed in proving to you that you will be able to [*repeat buying vision*], at that point, will you then introduce me to [*power person*]? Is that fair?" [*Get buyer's agreement and end call.*]	"When you ask me to prepare a proposal, I want you to know that it will contain no new information. It will simply document and confirm the business arrangements we will have discussed up to that point. [*Get buyer's agreement.*]
End call (write a Sponsor Letter)	I suggest (if we get that far) that I come out a week in advance of our delivery of the final proposal with a rough draft. We call this a pre-proposal review. There are two advantages to this approach. The advantage to you and your management team is that there will be no surprises in the final proposal; the advantage to me is that I can prepare the proposal correctly the first time." [*Get buyer's agreement and end call.*]
"Thank you for your time. I am going to consult with my resources. I will then write you a letter/e-mail confirming my understanding of your situation. In that letter, I will propose a specific way for us to prove these capabilities to you. You should receive that letter/e-mail shortly."	❑ End call (write a Power Sponsor Letter and Evaluation Plan)
	"Thank you for your time. I am going to take this list back with me. I will then make an initial attempt to put together a plan for you to evaluate our [*company/products/ services*]. You should receive the draft plan in a day or so. I will call you to discuss it."

Opportunity Assessment Worksheet

Overview

The Opportunity Assessment Worksheet is a qualification model consisting of 25 questions in five categories (pain, power, vision, value, and control). This scalable set of opportunity-focused questions helps you to objectively make an early (and continuing) qualification decision about whether to pursue an opportunity.

Where/How Used

The Opportunity Assessment Worksheet should be used to answer critical questions at strategic points in the life of an opportunity, including "Should we compete?" and "Can we win?"

What You Should Achieve

The user should answer the assessment honestly and objectively to determine

- What information is known
- What information is not known
- The scope of the activity and resources required to improve the status of the opportunity so that an engagement or disengagement decision can be made

Input Required

Information gained from conversations, research, and all known available data that might affect the current situation.

Opportunity Assessment Worksheet

Opportunity Assessment Worksheet		Assessment date: _____		
Answer key: (Y) Yes, (N) No, or (?) Unsure			Comp	
★ = "Quick Five" assessment questions		Us		
★	*Pain* "Is the customer likely to act?"	★		
1	Has high-priority pain or potential pain been identified?			
2	Have *we* validated the pain with the owner(s)?			
3	Do *we* understand how others are impacted by the pain?			
4	Is there a budget in place?			
5	Is there a time frame to address the pain?			
★	*Power* "Are *we* aligned with the right people to win?"	★		
6	Do *we* understand the roles of the key players for this opportunity?			
7	Do *we* understand who will influence the decision and how?			
8	Are *we* connected to the people in power?			
9	Do *we* have the support of the key players?			
10	Are *we* connected to the people with access to funds?			
★	*Vision* "Does the customer prefer *our* offering?"	★		
11	Did *we* help establish the initial requirements?			
12	Does *our* offering fit the customer's needs/requirements?			
13	Have *we* created or reengineered a differentiated vision for the key players?			
14	Do the key players support *our* solution approach?			
★	*Value* "Does *our* offering provide mutual value?"	★		
15	Do *we* understand the benefit to each key player and the corporation?			
16	Have the key players quantified and articulated the benefits of *our* offering to *us*?			
17	Has a (corporate) value analysis been agreed upon?			
18	Does the value analysis warrant access to funds?			
19	Is there sufficient value to *us*? Is the opportunity profitable? Is it strategic?			
★	*Control* "Can *we* control the buying process?"	★		
20	Do *we* understand the decision-making process and the criteria for the key players?			
21	Do *we* understand the proof and satisfaction requirements for the key players?			
22	Do *we* understand the customer's buying practices, policies, and procedures?			
23	Has the customer agreed to an evaluation process with *us*?			
24	Can *we* control the evaluation process?			
25	Can *we* successfully manage *our* risk?			

Competitive Strategy Selector

Overview

The Competitive Strategy Selector provides key questions that should be answered to direct the salesperson (and the account team) in selecting the competitive strategy to attempt to employ for the given opportunity, and also offers suggested supporting tactics.

Where/How Used

Depending on the opportunity's origin (i.e., a latent pain opportunity or an active opportunity), the strategy selected will vary. If the opportunity is latent, by default the team has engaged in a preemptive strategy. If the opportunity is of the active variety, the team should consider some key questions to determine exactly which competitive strategy (head-to-head, end around, divide and conquer, or stall) to use.

What You Should Achieve

You should be able to make a strategy decision. If the choice is to engage, then you should determine the strategy to use, determine specific tactics for executing the strategy, and weigh the pros and cons associated with the selected strategy and tactics. The chosen strategy should be communicated to the entire sales team.

Input Required

Enough knowledge of the account or opportunity origin to answer the initial key questions.

Competitive Strategy Selector

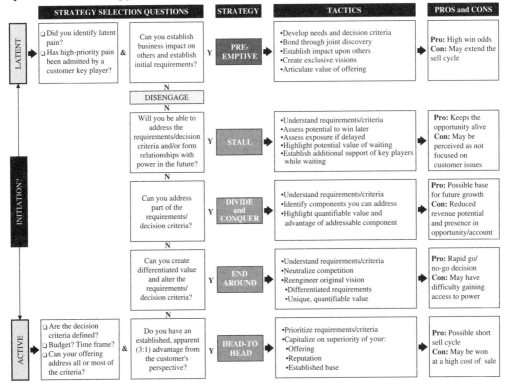

9 Block Vision Processing Model for Vision Creation

Overview

The 9 Block Vision Processing Model for Vision Creation is a buyer-focused questioning model used to diagnose an admitted pain and lead the buyer through self-conclusion to a vision of a solution.

Where/How Used

The framework of the 9 Block Vision Processing Model is derived by employing three types of questions:

- Open questions
- Control questions
- Confirming questions

These questions are used to cover three significant areas of exploration:

- Diagnosis of reasons for pain
- Exploration of the impact of pain on others
- Help in visualizing the capabilities needed

The 9 Block Vision Processing Model for Vision Creation is used when latent pain opportunities exist. You would navigate the model in a suggested sequence, leading the buyer to a buying vision.

Note: For active opportunities, you must reengineer a buyer's existing vision. This is done using the same model, but navigated in a different sequence. See Chapter 8, "How to Reengineer a Vision of a Solution."

What You Should Achieve

A successful use of the 9 Block Vision Processing Model for Vision Creation should result in the prospective buyer's developing a buying vision of how to address an admitted pain utilizing your capabilities. Both you and the buyer should have a clearer appreciation of the measurable value associated with resolving the buyer's pain. Also, both of you should have an understanding of the impact that the pain has across the buyer's organization.

Input Required

Pain Sheets are situationally specific job aids that help prompt a salesperson to ask intelligent, control-oriented questions in the control row of the 9 Block Vision Processing Model.

9 Block Vision Processing Model—Vision Creation

	DIAGNOSE REASONS	EXPLORE IMPACT	VISUALIZE CAPABILITIES
OPEN	R1 (1) "Tell me about it, what is causing you to have this... (repeat pain)?"	I1 (4) "Besides yourself, WHO in your organization is impacted by this (pain) and HOW are they impacted?"	C1 (7) "What is it going to take for YOU to be able to (achieve your goal)?" "Could I try a few ideas on you?"
CONTROL	R2 (2) "Is it because...?"	I2 (5) "Is this (pain) causing...?" "If so, would (title) also be concerned?"	C2 (8) "You mentioned (repeat reason) ...What if there were a way... *when, who, what* So that... ? ...would that help?
CONFIRM	R3 (3) "So, the reasons for your (repeat pain) are...? Is that correct?"	I3 (6) "From what I just heard... (repeat the WHO and HOW), it sounds like this is not just your problem, but a _____ problem! Is that correct?"	C3 (9) "So, IF you had the ability to (summarize capability visions), THEN could you (*achieve your goal*)?"

PAIN → ... → **BUYING VISION**

9 Block Vision Processing Model for Vision Reengineering

Overview

The 9 Block Vision Processing Model for Vision Reengineering is a buyer-focused questioning model. It is used to introduce differentiating capabilities while leading a buyer to self-conclusion of a reengineered vision of a solution.

Where/How Used

The framework of the 9 Block Vision Processing Model is derived by employing three types of questions:

- Open questions

- Control questions
- Confirming questions

These questions are used to cover three significant areas of exploration:

- Diagnosis of reasons for pain
- Exploration of the impact of pain on others
- Help in visualizing the capabilities needed

For active opportunities, a vision must be reengineered. You will need to navigate the model in a different sequence from that used in vision creation.

What You Should Achieve
Successful use of the 9 Block Vision Processing Model for Vision Reengineering should result in the prospective buyer's expanding or changing her or his original vision. If the new list of requirements includes your differentiated capabilities, then you have successfully reengineered the vision.

Input Required
Pain Sheets are situationally specific job aids that help prompt a salesperson to ask intelligent, control-oriented questions in the control row of the 9 Block Vision Processing Model. Pain Sheets used in Vision Reengineering should stress key differentiators.

9 Block Vision Processing Model—Vision Reengineering

	DIAGNOSE REASONS	EXPLORE IMPACT	VISUALIZE CAPABILITIES
OPEN	R1 (3) "How do you do 'it' today without this capability?"	I1 (6) "Besides yourself, WHO in your organization is impacted by this (pain) and HOW are they impacted?"	C1 (1) "How do you see yourself using this (repeat buyer initial vision)…?"
CONTROL	R2 (4) "Today…?"	I2 (7) "Is this (pain) causing…?" "If so, would (title) also be concerned?"	C2 (2) "Are you also looking for a way to…?" "Would it help if you also had a way to…?"
CONFIRM	R3 (5) "So, the way you do it today is… Is that correct?"	I3 (8) "From what I just heard… (repeat the WHO and HOW), it sounds like this is not just your problem, but a _____ problem! Is that correct?"	C3 (9) "…When you called, you were looking at (original "vision"). Today, you also said you needed… (capability visions). If you had…could you (verbalize goal)?"

PAIN → **CURRENT VISION**

↓ **BUYING VISION**

Pain Sheet

Overview

A Pain Sheet is a questioning prompter used with the 9 Block Vision Processing Model. It provides a set of control questions to help diagnose the reasons for a buyer's pain, identify the impacts of that pain on the rest of the organization, and describe the capabilities that could be provided to address the reasons for the pain. It is an integral job aid for creating (or reengineering) visions biased toward specific offerings or solutions of the selling organization.

Where/How Used
The Pain Sheet is used with the 9 Block Vision Processing Model to assist in asking questions that help you to create (or reengineer) a customer buying vision that is biased toward your specific offerings. The Pain Sheet can be used during conversations with buyers or prior to a meeting as a pre-call preparation aid.

What You Should Achieve
Asking the questions on a Pain Sheet should help you to

- Uncover reasons for the buyer's pain while biasing those reasons toward your offering

- Determine the quantifiable value of addressing the reasons by asking "drill-down" questions (also found on the Pain Sheet).

- Develop a view (or modify an existing view) of how the buyer's pain affects others throughout his or her organization (Pain Chain).

- Position your capabilities in a manner that clearly helps the buyer visualize how and what he or she will be able to do differently in the future

Input Required
To build a Pain Sheet, you will need an understanding of the prospect's (likely) pains, as well as associated reasons, and knowledge of how your capabilities can address the likely pains. Awareness of your differentiators will also be important.

Note: Ideally, a database of standard Pain Sheets cataloged by common pains, job titles, capabilities, and/or industries would be most useful. Additionally, existing Pain Sheets should be updated periodically and new ones should be constructed to coincide with the introduction of any new offering or capability.

Pain Sheet Template

<table>
<tr>
<td colspan="3">
Pain:
Job Title & Industry:
Offering:
</td>
</tr>
<tr>
<th>REASONS (R2)</th>
<th>IMPACT (I2)</th>
<th>CAPABILITIES (C2)</th>
</tr>
<tr>
<td>Is it because . . . ; Today . . . ?</td>
<td>Is this [pain] causing . . . ?</td>
<td>What if . . . ; Would it help if . . . ?</td>
</tr>
<tr>
<td>A.</td>
<td>
• _____ ?
• _____ ?
• _____ ?

Is the [<i>job title</i>] impacted?
</td>
<td>
A. When:
    Who:
    What:
</td>
</tr>
<tr>
<td>B.</td>
<td>
• _____ ?
• _____ ?
• _____ ?

Is the [<i>job title</i>] impacted?
</td>
<td>
B. When:
    Who:
    What:
</td>
</tr>
<tr>
<td>C.</td>
<td>
• _____ ?
• _____ ?
• _____ ?

Is the [<i>job title</i>] impacted?
</td>
<td>
C. When:
    Who:
    What:
</td>
</tr>
<tr>
<td>D.</td>
<td></td>
<td>
D. When:
    Who:
    What:
</td>
</tr>
</table>

RFP Initial Response Letter

Overview
The RFP Initial Response Letter is a letter or e-mail sent by you that attempts to suggest a bargain in which you will respond to the RFP in exchange for first meeting with the key players impacted by the scope of the project.

Where/How Used
The RFP Initial Response Letter is used only after the RFP sender has denied a verbal request by you to meet with the customer key players impacted by the scope of the project

The RFP Initial Response Letter is used to document your request and to make a calculated statement to the buyer that suggests that your organization has a practice of responding to RFPs only after you've met with the key players impacted by the project, and that this practice is in the best interest of the buyer's organization.

What You Should Achieve
The RFP Initial Response Letter should achieve one of two results:

1. You are granted access to the desired key players in order to conduct vision processing interviews.

2. The RFP sender responds with a final denial, at which point you have to decide whether to respond to the RFP or to disengage.

Input Required
The key input will be deciding which of the key players will need to be interviewed.

Note: This approach should be supported by senior executives within your organization because it challenges traditional approaches to handling RFPs.

RFP Initial Response Letter Template

Dear _____ [*RFP sender*]

Thank you for the opportunity to propose to your organization. We appreciate your confidence in us.

As I mentioned on the phone, our practice is not to respond to Requests for Proposal until we have personally interviewed the department heads impacted by the scope of the project. We have found that this practice enables us to do more complete work on behalf of our potential clients, resulting in a more satisfactory implementation of the project. The client is the major beneficiary of this practice.

If you would arrange for us to meet with _____ [*title**], _____ [*title**], and _____ [*title**] for [*one*] hour each, we will then invest the time and resources to respond to the RFP to your satisfaction.

In the meantime, I have enclosed some detailed information on our products and services. If you have any further questions, don't hesitate to call.

Sincerely,

_____

*These job titles are determined after evaluating the scope of the RFP.

RFP Executive Summary

Overview

The RFP Executive Summary highlights additional capabilities needed by the buying organization that are not found in the scope of its current RFP.

Where/How Used

The RFP Executive Summary is sent to the RFP sender and the key players met with during the interviews (negotiated via the RFP Initial Response Letter). The RFP Executive Summary should be placed at the beginning of the RFP response or used as a cover letter that accompanies the final proposal.

The RFP Executive Summary summarizes additional capabilities needed by the key players that were uncovered during the vision processing conversations that took place during the agreed-upon interviews.

What You Should Achieve

The intent of the RFP Executive Summary is to stress the importance of the additional capabilities needed from the perspective of the key players. The desire is to catch the attention of the RFP sender and/or consultant(s) in order to have the initial requirements of the RFP expanded or changed to include these additional capabilities.

Input Required

The critical input into the RFP Executive Summary is the highlighting of your differentiating capabilities needed by the key players.

RFP Executive Summary Template

Dear _____ [RFP sender or consultant],

Thank you for arranging our meeting with _____ [title*],
_____ [title*], and _____ [title*].
Their input proved to be invaluable in the preparation of our response.

Attached is our response to your RFP. Based on our interviews, _____
[#] primary capabilities are sought by these executives:

I have highlighted those capabilities that are within the RFP (out of the
_____ [total #] questions).

Capability 1: _____
Capability 2: _____
Capability 3: _____
Capability 4: _____
Etc.

I have added _____ [#] capabilities that were outside the scope of the
RFP as numbers _____, _____, and _____ [etc.]. The executives
interviewed said that these specific capabilities should also be included in
the RFP.

Capability 5: _____
Capability 6: _____
Capability 7: _____
Etc.

Again, thank you for the opportunity to propose our products/services to
your client. I look forward to working with you toward a successful
implementation of these capabilities.

Sincerely,

_____

cc: _____ [customer key player(s) with whom you had the best rapport]

*These job titles were interviewed as a result of the RFP Initial Response Letter.

Sponsor Letter (or e-mail) for Vision Creation

Overview
The Sponsor Letter for Vision Creation is a letter or e-mail sent to the prospective buyer that documents and confirms a buying vision that you created. The letter further confirms the buyer's intention to introduce you to the potential power sponsor. In essence, the Sponsor Letter is confirmation of the conversation you had.

Where/How Used
The Sponsor Letter for Vision Creation contains six key elements from discussions with the sponsor, summarized in your words. The elements are

1. Pain

2. Reasons for pain

3. Capabilities needed (buying vision)

4. Agreement to explore further

5. Bargain for access to power

6. Suggested proof step—what you offered in return for access to power

What You Should Achieve

- A mutual understanding of what was discussed during the vision creation conversation. If the potential sponsor does not agree with the elements of the letter, you are able to find this out before proceeding.

- The sponsor perceives you as thorough, organized, and professional.

- Access to power.

Input Required

To create the Sponsor Letter, you need details on the sponsor's pain, the reasons for the pain, the buying vision created, and options to offer as proof.

Sponsor Letter (or e-mail) for Vision Creation Template

Dear _____ [*sponsor's name*],

Thank you for your interest in _____ [*your company*]. The purpose of this letter is to summarize my understanding of our meeting and our action plan.

We discussed the following:

Your primary critical issue is _____.

Reasons you are having this critical business issue are

Reason A: _____
Reason B: _____
Reason C: _____

Capabilities you said you needed to resolve this situation are

Capability A: _____
Capability B: _____
Capability C: _____

Our next steps:

You agreed to move forward with our company, and you said that if we succeed in proving we can give you these capabilities, you will introduce me to _____ [*power sponsor name and title*]. You mentioned that *he/she* is not happy with the impact that [*your critical business issue*] is having upon *his/her* ability to _____.

I would like to propose that _____
_____
[*describe the proof step needed if it is part of a bargain for access to power*].

I am confident that you will like what you see and will introduce our company to the rest of your organization. I'll call you on _____ to discuss it further.

Sincerely,

_____

Sponsor Letter (or e-mail) for Vision Reengineering

Overview

The Sponsor Letter for Vision Reengineering is a letter or e-mail you send that documents and confirms a new buying vision that you reengineered with a potential sponsor. The letter further confirms the buyer's intention to introduce you to the potential power sponsor. In essence, the sponsor letter is confirmation of the conversation you had during and after vision reengineering.

Where/How Used

The Sponsor Letter for Vision Reengineering contains six key elements from discussions with the sponsor, summarized in your words. The elements are

1. Prospect's original vision

2. Salesperson's additional capabilities

3. Expanded buying vision

4. Reasons and resulting pain

5. Organizational impact and access to power

6. Proof requirement of all vendors

What You Should Achieve

- A mutual understanding of what was discussed during the vision reengineering conversation. If the potential sponsor does not agree with the elements of the letter, you are able to find this out before proceeding.

- The sponsor perceives you as thorough, organized, and professional.

- Access to power.

Input Required

To create the Sponsor Letter, you need specific details on the sponsor's pain, the reasons for the pain, the impact of the pain on others, and the customer's original buying vision.

Sponsor Letter (or e-mail) for Vision Reengineering Template

Dear _____ [*sponsor's name*],

Thank you for your interest in _____ [*your company*]. The purpose of this letter is to summarize my understanding of our meeting and our action plan.

Capabilities you said you needed: When we began our conversation, you were looking for the ability to [*describe original capabilities needed*]
Capability A: _____,

As our conversation progressed, you also told me you needed a way to [*describe additional capabilities needed*]
Capability B: _____
Capability C: _____
Capability D: _____

You said that if you had these capabilities, you could better address your critical business issue of _____.

Reasons you are having this critical business issue are

Reason A: _____,
Reason B: _____,
Reason C: _____,
Reason D: _____.

Our next steps:

You agreed to move forward with our company, and you said that if we succeed in proving that we can give you these capabilities, you will introduce me to _____ [*power sponsor name and title*]. You mentioned that *he/she* is not happy with the impact that [*your critical business issue*] is having upon *his/her* ability to _____.

At that meeting we can mutually agree on appropriate next steps. As we discussed, I will be required to provide proof that we can give you these capabilities, and you will require that proof of all other potential consultants. I look forward to our next meeting on _____.

Sincerely,

_____

Power Sponsor Letter
(or e-mail)

Overview

The Power Sponsor Letter is a letter or e-mail you send that documents and confirms a buying vision that you helped create with a potential power sponsor. The Power Sponsor Letter is similar to the Sponsor Letter in both style and content, with the exception that an Evaluation Plan is attached with the Power Sponsor Letter. In essence, the Power Sponsor Letter is a confirmation of the conversation you had during vision processing.

Where/How Used

The Power Sponsor Letter contains six key elements from discussions with the power sponsor, summarized in your words. Those elements are

1. Pain

2. Reasons for pain

3. Capabilities needed (buying vision)

4. Organizational impact

5. Agreement to explore further

6. Evaluation Plan

What You Should Achieve

- A mutual understanding of what was discussed during the vision processing conversation. If the potential power sponsor does not agree with the elements of the letter, you are able to find that out before proceeding so that corrective actions can be taken.

- The power sponsor perceives you as thorough, organized, and professional.

Input Required

To create the Power Sponsor Letter, you need specific details on the power sponsor's pain, the reasons for the pain, and the buying vision created, and you need to be able to articulate the impact of the power sponsor's pain on others in the organization.

Power Sponsor Letter (or e-mail) Template

Dear _____ [*power sponsor's name*],

Thank you for meeting with _____ [*sponsor's name*] and me earlier today. I believe it was time well spent for both of our organizations.

We discussed the following:

Your primary critical issue is _____.

Reasons you are having this critical business issue are

Reason A: _____,
Reason B: _____,
Reason C: _____,

Capabilities you said you needed to resolve this situation are

Capability A: _____
Capability B: _____
Capability C: _____

Our next steps:

When I told you I was confident that our organization can help you to _____ [*describe goal of power sponsor*], you agreed to take a serious look at our ability to do so. Based on my knowledge to date, I am suggesting an evaluation plan for your further exploration of our organization's capabilities. Look over the plan with _____ [*sponsor*], and I will call you on _____ to get your thoughts.

Sincerely,

_____

Attachment:
Draft Evaluation Plan

Evaluation Plan

Overview
The Evaluation Plan is a job aid used in conjunction with the Power Sponsor Letter. It outlines the suggested steps that you want to be followed.

Where/How Used
The Evaluation Plan captures events that you and power sponsors can agree upon. You assign dates to each event with the thought of closing the sale on an agreed-upon date. This helps to control and shorten sales cycles. The Evaluation Plan should be a mutually owned project plan.

What You Should Achieve
The Evaluation Plan should help you maintain control of the buying process by documenting all events that will take place during the course of the sale and the sequence in which those events will take place. By managing this plan with a buyer, you can predict when resources will be needed and anticipate potential hurdles to closure of the sale. Changes to the draft plan made by power sponsors are an indication of ownership and "buy-in" to the approach.

Input Required
To create an Evaluation Plan, you need to know the buyer's criteria for buying and to have an understanding of your company's recommended approach for evaluation. Some other things that you should consider include

- Month-end, quarter-end, year-end, and other periodic events
- Whether or not any of the events should be billable
- The time required to accomplish each event
- Resources needed to execute the events in the plan

Evaluation Plan Template

[DRAFT]					
Event	Week Of	✓	Responsible	Go/No-Go	Billable
*Indicates a "go/no-go" mutual decision to be made.					

Go/No-Go Step
Completion Letter (or e-mail)

Overview

The Go/No-Go Step Completion Letter is sent to the power sponsor or some other person responsible for executing the steps of the Evaluation Plan. The intent is to confirm that a go/no-go step on the Evaluation Plan has been completed.

Where/How Used

The Go/No-Go Step Completion Letter should be used after completing any event designated as a go/no-go decision on the Evaluation Plan. Other customer individuals involved in the decision-making process can be copied on the letter or e-mail. The completion letter simply advises all parties involved of the steps completed, when the steps were completed, and which step(s) will be taken next.

What You Should Achieve

The Go/No-Go Step Completion Letter can ensure that everyone involved in the opportunity is informed of and in alignment with the progress of the plan's execution. Also, it can serve as an indicator of additional time and resources that may be necessary.

Input Required

To create the Go/No-Go Step Completion Letter, the development of an Evaluation Plan must be completed, with events or steps, go/no-go decision points, and dates assigned.

Note: The Go/No-Go Step Completion Letter is a simple, yet powerful way to stay in front of the customer on a regular basis. You also may want to include or attach the updated Evaluation Plan showing any changes to the plan as well as the events that have been marked as completed.

Go/No-Go Step Completion Letter (or e-mail) Template

Dear _____ [*power sponsor's name or person executing the evaluation plan*],

I am pleased to report that another milestone has been completed. On _____ [*date*] we accomplished _____ [*describe event accomplished*].

Our next milestone is the week of _____ [*date*], when *we* are scheduled to _____ [*describe event to be accomplished*].

Thank you again for your continued support of this project.

Sincerely,

_____

cc: _____

_____

_____

[*copy appropriate individuals*]

Attachment:
Updated Evaluation Plan

Value Justification Model

Overview

A Value Justification Model is used to document and present the projected benefits associated with the use of your products and services after implementation. The projected, quantifiable benefits are presented in relation to the total investment being made by the buying organization.

Where/How Used

A Value Justification Model is usually presented during the proof phase of a selling cycle. It provides a detailed breakdown of the projected benefits (profit and revenue increases and cost decreases) to the buyer's organization. The schedule of investments (one-time and ongoing) to be made by the buyer is also explained.

Note: Success in using Value Justification Models is recognized when the metrics of the analysis are derived from and owned by the buyer. These metrics are usually derived from your vision processing conversations with the buyers.

What You Should Achieve

Using a Value Justification Model will clearly define the potential value to be received by both you and the buyer. This provides you with logical reasons to give fewer concessions during negotiations. It also gives the buyer a compelling reason to take action.

Input Required

Completion of a Value Justification Model requires you to know the estimated customer investment for the entire project, the projected benefits associated with the use of the implemented offerings, and a reasonable prediction of when benefits can begin to be realized.

Note: Exercise caution when using the term *ROI* (return on investment), since most buyers have their own definition of what that means.

Value Justification Model Worksheet
Phased over Time (in 000s)

	Q1	Q2	Q3	Q4
BENEFITS				
Increased profit from increased revenue				
Reduced cost				
Avoided cost				
Quarterly total				
Cumulative value				
INVESTMENTS				
One-time investment				
Ongoing investment				
Quarterly total				
Cumulative investment				
NET VALUE				
Quarterly total				
Cumulative total				

Sources of data:

First-year net return: $_____
Breakeven point: Q_____
ROI (first year):   _____%

Success Criteria

Overview

Success Criteria establish the baseline metrics for measuring the effectiveness and value of your capabilities in the prospective buyer's organization.

Where/How Used

Success Criteria should be mutually defined and agreed upon during the evaluation process. After delivery of your solution to the customer, you should measure the Success Criteria on an ongoing basis and report the results to the customer.

What You Should Achieve

- Higher levels of customer satisfaction, as the customer understands the value of the solutions you have provided
- Credibility for you and your company
- Additional business from future projects

Input Required

To create the initial Success Criteria, the buying and selling organizations should agree on the current baseline metrics to be measured. They also should determine how often each metric will be measured (e.g., monthly, quarterly, or semiannually).

Note: You should ensure that the Success Criteria can be attributed to your offerings. Success Criteria that are too broad may allow outside factors to affect the results.

Success Criteria Template

Success Criteria	Baseline	Q1	Q2	Q3	Q4
Sources of data:					

Negotiating Worksheet

Overview

The Negotiating Worksheet is used as a prenegotiation preparation tool. It helps you resist requests for concessions that are likely to be made by the buyer.

Where/How Used

The Negotiating Worksheet should be completed prior to discussions to finalize the terms of the sale. It provides guidelines for making stands against buyer concessions. The stands should be based on logical information that you developed during the buying process. Key "stands" may include (in no particular order of importance)

1. *Pain stand* Recall the buyer's pain that is driving the opportunity.

2. *Vision stand* Recall the vision established to address the critical business issue.

3. *Value stand* Recall the quantifiable value associated with addressing the pain.

4. *Plan stand* Recall the Evaluation Plan, indicating the timeline to realize benefits.

What You Should Achieve

- Reduced stress by minimizing the pressure on you to discount your price or give in on terms

- Higher margins

- Fewer concessions

- Improved negotiations

- Better business terms and conditions

Input Required

To create the Negotiating Worksheet, pain must have been uncovered, a buying vision created, a Value Justification Model completed, and an Evaluation Plan with a planned implementation date agreed upon.

Negotiating Worksheet Template

Is it closable today?	___ Power to buy? ___ Payback agreed to? ___ L/T/A approvals? ___ Plan completed? ___ Known cost since	_____ _____ _____	Prepared for: ___ Price? ___ Terms? ___ Risk?

Stand 1:
PLAN

"Our published plan shows an implementation starting on
_____ [*date*]. Is this issue worth the delay?"

Stand 2:
VALUE

"When we calculated the payback, you said
_____.
We agreed that the project would pay for itself in ___ months."

Stand 3:
PAIN

"The reason we have spent the last ___ months together is
because _____.
That issue will not go away until you gain these new capabilities."

Stand 4:
VISION

"You told me that you needed a way to [*when, who, what*]
_____.
As you know, we can provide you that capability."

"The only way I could do something for you is if you could do something for me."
Buyer should ask: *"Like what?"*

Note: Prepare a Give-Get List to help determine the "gets" and "gives" below.

Is it possible for you to:
_____?
Is that possible?

SILENCE! ONLY if buyer accepts your condition . . .

If you can _____**, then we are**
prepared to
_____,
which is worth $_____.

Can we go forward on that basis?

Anxiety Creation

Overview
Anxiety Creation is a technique that creates a plausible problem or situation that can be readily solved with your capabilities. It usually can serve to set up a differentiating capability.

Where/How Used
Anxiety Creation is typically used when you engage with a buyer who has already established a vision—usually one with a competitor's capabilities. Your differentiators are then positioned using the anxiety technique to create an "I must have that!" condition. Getting a prospect to this state of mind is necessary in order to change the requirements and rules that have already been established for active opportunities (and currently are not in your favor).

What You Should Achieve
As a result of using Anxiety Creation, you should be able to incorporate specific differentiating capabilities into a buyer's already established vision. This technique, incorporated in Vision Reengineering, serves to change the rules of the decision and bias them in your favor.

Input Required
Situational knowledge of the client's business, as well as corresponding knowledge of past clients in related industries and the results they achieved with your solution or specific capability.

Note: Anxiety Creation is also a useful technique to incorporate into marketing messages and other business development approaches. It is also an effective technique for positioning your capabilities during vision creation.

Anxiety Creation Example

Situation:

Job Title: VP Sales   **Industry:** manufacturing company

Anxiety Question:

"How would you feel if . . .

. . . you just received a call from your largest customer, and they told you they were going to switch to one of your competitors? They said the reason was that they rarely could get answers to questions on delivery and back-order status, special pricing arrangements, etc. It put them at a competitive disadvantage with their own customers. They mentioned that your competitor provided answers to those important questions immediately."

Capability Question:

"What if there was a way that . . .

. . . when key customers require answers to critical, frequently asked questions (FAQs), they could use a standard Web browser to make inquiries and get immediate responses while maintaining the highest levels of security, so that your salespeople could spend less time answering FAQs and more time prospecting for new accounts?"

Feature and/or Offering:

"The Customer Preferences feature of our e-commerce offering can give you that capability."

Anxiety Creation Worksheet

Situation:

Job Title: _____   Industry: _____

Anxiety Question:

"How would you feel if . . .

_____
_____
_____
_____
_____ ?"

Capability Question:

"What if there was a way that . . .

_____
_____
_____
_____
_____ ?"

Feature and/or Offering:

 ## Transition Issues and Capabilities Worksheet

Overview

The Transition Issues and Capabilities Worksheet is a document that outlines the primary transition issues experienced by the person within the buying organization who is responsible for implementing your operational capabilities. It also describes potential reasons for the transition issues and your corresponding transition capabilities or services that address them.

Where/How Used

A transition issue (pain) normally arises when a customer individual is given the task of implementing operational capabilities desired by a particular line of business within the buying organization. Although the person responsible for implementation may be interested in helping the organization, that person may feel hindered when it comes to making it happen. The hindrance usually revolves around

- *Lack of time* An extensive list of projects and tasks already occupies the person's limited time, and any other projects are seen as adding to the load.

- *Lack of resources* The personnel required to accomplish the transition doesn't currently reside in the buyer's organization.

- *Lack of skills* The person or team responsible for implementation doesn't have the expertise necessary to make the transition occur.

What You Should Achieve

This worksheet provides an opportunity for you to create a transition vision for the person responsible for implementation. This "additional sale" can also help minimize the perceived risk associated with implementing the operational capabilities.

Input Required

You need to anticipate potential transition pains, understand possible steps that the implementation team may need to take in order to ensure a successful implementation of the operational capabilities, and know your service capabilities.

Note: A Transition Issues and Capabilities Worksheet provides the basis for building a Pain Sheet to be used with the person responsible for implementation. The use of it tends to come later in a sell cycle (after the "operational" sale has been made). It usually focuses on a particular department that will be responsible for making the transition from a current state of business to the new state as a result of the operational sale.

Transition Issues and Capabilities Worksheet Example

Job Title (person responsible for implementation):
John Watkins, CIO

Transition Issue/Pain:
Delays implementing the e-commerce application on schedule

REASONS		TRANSITION CAPABILITIES
A. The technical staff lacks the time and resources to devote to a new system.	⇔	**A.** One week after agreement to proceed, our programmers can begin customizing an e-commerce application supervised by the customer's staff.
B. Available packages do not integrate with existing applications.	⇔	**B.** 60 days prior to cut-over, our consultants can guide your programmers to create interfaces with existing applications.
C. Limited training resources.	⇔	**C.** Two weeks prior to cut-over, one of our business partners can be contracted for salesperson training, so your IT staff can concentrate on integrating the application.

Transition Issues and Capabilities Worksheet

Job Title (person responsible for implementation):
_____

Transition Issue/Pain:
_____

REASONS		TRANSITION CAPABILITIES
A.	⇔	A.
B.	⇔	B.
C.	⇔	C.

Implementation Plan Letter (or e-mail)

Overview

The Implementation Plan Letter serves as a cover letter for the Proposed Implementation Plan itself. Much like the Power Sponsor Letter confirms the vision processing conversation you had with power and introduces the Evaluation Plan, the Implementation Plan Letter confirms the transition vision of the person responsible for implementation and introduces the Implementation (Transition) Plan.

Where/How Used

The Implementation Plan Letter is intended to summarize and document the information uncovered in a transition vision processing conversation. Key content should include the primary transition issue (pain), the reasons for the issue, transition capabilities and services suggested, and introduction of the Proposed Implementation (Transition) Plan.

What You Should Achieve

The Implementation Plan Letter will serve as a cover letter for the actual plan as well as a summary of the conversation that led to the development of the plan. The letter should successfully introduce the plan while gaining agreement to the content of the transition vision processing conversation.

Input Required

A well-written Implementation Plan Letter requires an understanding of the buyer's potential transition issues, reasons for each issue, service capabilities that will help address the issues, and the steps the implementation team will need to take in order to ensure a successful implementation in the buyer's organization.

Implementation Plan Letter (or e-mail) Example

Dear John,

Thank you for your participation in discussing the implementation of e-commerce at TGI. The purpose of this letter is to summarize my understanding of our meeting and propose some transition assistance for you.

We discussed the following:

Concern about potential delays in meeting an aggressive implementation schedule. Your current backlog for new applications is nine months, largely due to budget restrictions and because your programmers spend about 80 percent of their time maintaining legacy applications. Your specific areas of concern as they relate to the schedule are

- Enhancements must be made to an existing, proven e-commerce software package to meet TGI's unique needs.
- The new system must be integrated with your existing accounting and inventory applications.
- Your Director of Training is concerned that training and documentation will require significant resources.

Proposed Transition Capabilities

- One week after agreement to proceed, our programmers will begin customizing the e-commerce application, supervised by your staff.
- 60 days prior to cut-over, our consultants will guide your programmers to create interfaces to mesh with existing applications.
- Two weeks prior to cut-over, a recommended business partner could be contracted for salesperson and customer training, so that your IT staff can concentrate on integrating the application.

You said that if you had these capabilities, you could support the proposed e-commerce implementation.

Our next steps

You indicated that final approval of funding would be with Jim Smith, your Vice President of Finance, and you agreed to set up a meeting for the three of us to review our recommendations. Based on my knowledge to date, I am suggesting an implementation plan for your consideration. Look it over with Jim, and we can review it on March 18 when we will be helping Jim analyze the value of the project.

Sincerely,
Bill Hart

Attachment:
Implementation Plan

Implementation Plan Letter (or e-mail) Template

Dear _____ [*name of person responsible for implementation*],

Thank you for your participation in discussing the implementation of _____ [*description of operational offering/capabilities*]. The purpose of this letter is to summarize my understanding of our meeting and propose some transition assistance to you.

We discussed the following:

Your primary concern about implementing the operational capabilities your organization seeks is _____.

The reasons you are having this transition issue are

Reason A: _____,
Reason B: _____,
Reason C: _____.

The transition capabilities you said you needed to resolve this situation include

Capability A: _____,
Capability B: _____,
Capability C: _____.

You said that if you had these capabilities, you could support the implementation of the desired operational capabilities.

Our next steps:

You suggested that _____ [*power sponsor and/or financial approver*] would be responsible for approving the funding of these services. Based on my knowledge to date, I am attaching a proposed implementation plan for your consideration. If you (and anyone else necessary) would initially review it, then we can discuss it together on _____ [*date*].

I look forward to helping you implement these capabilities and services within your organization.

Sincerely,

_____

Attachment:
Implementation Plan

Implementation (Transition) Plan

Overview

The Implementation Plan is sent with the Implementation Plan Letter to the individual or group within the buying organization that is responsible for implementation.

Where/How Used

The Implementation Plan outlines, on a step-by-step basis, the actions that will have to be taken to alleviate the concerns the buyer has regarding the adaptation of the operational capabilities to the buying organization's environment. It also details who will be responsible (you or the buyer) for the steps/tasks that need to be completed, when they need to be completed, and whether each step is billable or not.

What You Should Achieve

Agreeing on the content of the Implementation Plan creates alignment between the buyer and your implementation team. This helps lead to a predictable and comfortable transition while minimizing the perceived risk of supporting the operational sale that has been made.

Input Required

To complete an Implementation Plan, an understanding of both the steps in the plan and the resources needed to execute those steps will be needed. The Implementation Plan should align its activities so that it delivers expected benefits in a time frame that has been agreed upon.

Proposed Implementation (Transition) Plan Example

Week Of	Event	Responsibility		Billable
		Us	Client	
May 10	Kickoff meeting—finalize success criteria	X	X	
May 17	Begin design enhancements to e-commerce software package	X		$250K
June 7	Create customer interfaces from the online order entry system to accounting and inventory systems	X	X	$250K
June 12	Run pilot		X	
June 19	Review pilot results with management team	X	X	
June 24	Finalize the field sales/customer cut-over plan	X	X	
Aug. 1–28	Field sales cut-over—90% of sales staff		X	
Oct. 1– Nov. 10	Consultants accompany TGI representatives to teach customers how to place their orders online	X	X	$42K
Dec. 31, Mar. 31, June 30, Sept. 30	Perform customer satisfaction and success criteria review	X	X	

Proposed Implementation (Transition) Plan Template

Week Of	Event	Responsibility		Billable
		Us	Client	

Solution Selling Pipeline Milestones

Milestone	Milestone Description	Sales Activities
—T—	Territory	☐ Opportunity identified in territory
—S—	Qualified Suspect	☐ Meets marketing criteria ☐ Potential sponsor identified ☐ Initial contact established (verifiable)
—D—	Qualified Sponsor	☐ Pain admitted by sponsor ☐ Sponsor has a valued buying vision ☐ Sponsor agreed to explore ☐ Access to power negotiated ☐ Agreed to above in Sponsor Letter
—C—	Qualified Power Sponsor	☐ Access to power sponsor ☐ Pain admitted by power sponsor ☐ Power sponsor has a valued buying vision ☐ Power sponsor agreed to explore ☐ Evaluation Plan proposed ☐ Evaluation Plan agreed upon
		☐ Evaluation Plan underway ☐ Pre-proposal review conducted ☐ Asked for the business ☐ Proposal issued, decision due ☐ Verbal approval received
—B—	Decision Due	☐ Contract negotiation in progress
—A—	Pending Sale	☐ Signed documents
—W—	Win	☐ Update prospect database

Pipeline Milestone Worksheet

Days in Code	Opportunity Name →	1	2	3	4	5	6	7	8	9	10	
												Latent or active opportunity (L-A)
												Potential sale amount ($K)
T												Opportunity identified in territory
												Meets marketing criteria
												Potential sponsor identified
S												Initial contact established (verifiable)
												Pain admitted by sponsor
												Sponsor has a valued buying vision
												Sponsor agreed to explore
												Access to power negotiated
D												Agreed to above in Sponsor Letter
												Access to power sponsor
												Pain admitted by power sponsor
												Power sponsor has a valued buying vision
												Power sponsor agreed to explore
												Evaluation Plan proposed
C												Evaluation Plan agreed upon
												Evaluation Plan underway
												Pre-proposal review conducted
												Asked for the business
												Proposal issued, decision due*
B												Verbal approval received
A												Contract negotiation in process
W												Signed documents
												Update prospect database

*Premature delivery of a proposal may *not* be a sign of progress.

Typical Time in Code Table

Milestone	Sell Cycle Length in Months					
	3 months	4 months	6 months	8 months	9 months	12 months
S	9	15	15	15	15	15
D	18	24	30	30	35	40
C	30	42	90	150	170	250
B	18	24	30	30	35	40
A	11	11	11	11	11	11
W	4	4	4	4	4	4

Pipeline Analysis Worksheet

A	Quota:					
B	Average sell time:					
C	Average size of opportunities ($)					
D	Current month:					
E	Year-to-date attainment not reflected in Ws ($):					
F	Milestone Code		Revenue	×	Win Odds	Yield
	S	$		×	10%	= $
	D	$		×	25%	= $
	C	$		×	50%	= $
	B	$		×	75%	= $
	A	$		×	90%	= $
	W	$		×	100%	= $
					Total yield in pipeline:	$
G	Revenue underway (E + F):					$
H	Shortfall to go (A − G):					$
I	Likely additional yield (F ÷ B × number of months left to sell):					$
J	Remaining shortfall to go (H − I):					$
K	New Ss required (J ÷ C × 10):					

INDEX